FINDING
THE GOOD

LUCAS L. JOHNSON II

Rutledge Hill Press™
Nashville, Tennessee

A Division of Thomas Nelson, Inc.
www.ThomasNelson.com

Published by Rutledge Hill Press, a Division of Thomas Nelson, Inc., P.O. Box 141000, Nashville, Tennessee 37214.

Library of Congress Cataloging-in-Publication Data

Johnson, Lucas, 1969–
     Finding the good / by Lucas Johnson.
         p. cm.
     ISBN 1-4016-0037-9 (hardcover)
     1. Montgomery, Fred, 1916– 2. African Americans-Tennessee-Henning-Biography. 3. Historians-Tennessee-Henning-Biography. 4. Mayors-Tennessee-Henning-Biography. 5. Henning (Tenn.)—Biography. 6. Henning (Tenn.)—Race relations. 7. African Americans-Tennessee-Henning-Social conditions—20th century. 8. Haley, Alex-Friends and associates. 9. Haley, Alex-Homes and haunts-Tennessee-Henning. 10. Johnson, Lucas, 1969- I. Title.
F444.H44J64 2003
976.8'16--dc21   2003007752

Printed in the United States of America
03 04 05 06 07—5 4 3 2 1

Contents

This book is dedicated to my grandmother,
Gladys Johnson,
and in memory of her husband,
my grandfather, Leroy.

Acknowledgments

Not one word of this book could have been written without God's guidance. Each day, before my fingers touched the keyboard, I prayed for wisdom and perseverance. Thanks for answering my prayer.

I want to thank my family for all their support; : my grandmother for her's prayers and, my mother, and father,, and especially my two sisters—Cathy and Stephanie—for listening patiently as I read excerpts of the book over the telephone,. and responding honestly. Your criticism was well received. Enormous thanks goes to Terrie Williams for helping me put this story in the right hands. I am also grateful to my agent, Joann Davis, whose diligence and expertise made it all happen, and to my editor at Rutledge Hill Press,, JGeoff Stone, whose ideas made the book better.and the rest of the Rutledge Hill family. Thanks also to Larry, Terri, Bryan and Tracey of the Rutledge Hill family. All of you assisted me in some way. I am very appreciative to those members of my blood family whose lives I discuss in the book in some capacity. You are inspirations, and I know what I've said about you will touch the lives of others. Thanks to my colleagues at The Associated Press, and others in the field of journalism, whose guidance over the years helped me become a better writer. There are many others who were supportive during the writing of this book. I can't forget Rhonda, whose sweet voice encouraged me when I grew tired, and reminded me that such a book is needed today. And I'm extremely grateful to Robbie, Jacques, and Lawrence, who helped a brother when he needed most. To the three of you, I say, "A-Phi!"

But most of all, thank you Fred Montgomery for allowing me to tell your story. Thank you for having faith in me. Thank you for *finding the good* in me.

As for the great storyteller himself, Alex Haley, thanks for providing the *Rroots*, from which I was able to grow.

Rest in peace.

INTRODUCTION

Darkness cannot drive out darkness;
only light can do that.
Hate cannot drive out hate;
only love can do that.
—MARTIN LUTHER KING JR.

I remember when I got the freelance assignment. It was a slow news day at the Nashville, Tennessee, Associated Press bureau, and I was shooting the breeze with coworker Joe Edwards. A friendly, easygoing guy, Joe seemed always to have my best interests at heart, and I kind of looked up to him. After all, he'd been there more than thirty years, longer than anyone on the editorial staff. He could have been chief of bureau somewhere if he wanted. But knowing Joe, he just didn't want the headache. He liked things steady and routine—to go home to his lovely wife, Sandra, and their dog, Emmitt. On this particular day, Joe told me he'd received a call from one of his contacts at the Tennessee Tourism Department about a national tourism magazine that was looking for someone to do a feature story on the Alex Haley Museum in Henning. Joe said he thought the assignment would be perfect for me and gave me the magazine contact. Shamefully, I must admit that I'd never heard of the museum before, but I did know Haley was from Henning. When I talked to the editor at *Friendly Exchange*, she gave me details about the assignment and told me I might want to pay close attention to the museum's curator, and that's about all she said about him. At the time, I didn't care to know too much more, except maybe how much I was getting paid.

Henning, located about fifty miles north of Memphis, has a population of roughly twelve hundred, about 60 percent black. Just before Henning are Covington and Ripley, two slightly larger towns. As a child, I remember going to a Methodist church in Covington when my mother's denomination would have youth conferences during the summer. But I had no idea what was beyond Covington. Needless to say, on my way to Henning for the assignment, I was reminded of the meandering country roads we had to travel. As I turned each curve, I thought about my childhood and the bumps I encountered.

I was raised in a rough part of Memphis, Tennessee, called Orange Mound. The neighborhood wasn't that bad when we moved there in 1969. But like many black communities in the late seventies and early eighties, it grew progressively worse as cocaine came on the drug scene. Dope houses began to crop up on both sides of my street, and drug dealers were the entrepreneurs of the community. As violence grew within its borders, the Mound became notorious in the South, much like Los Angeles's Compton. My friends embraced the tough reputation. Most of them fatherless, they dreamed of emulating the lifestyle of the dealers, who kept rolls of hundreds in their pockets and drove flashy cars. Still boys, they had chosen the path they thought led to manhood.

My mother, Shirley, is a petite, hardworking woman who almost single-handedly raised my two older sisters and me. She did her best to shelter me. She walked me to the bus stop nearly every day till she thought I was big enough to take care of myself. Even though she had only a high school diploma, my mother had a Ph.D. in sewing. She worked at that machine sometimes from sunup to sundown to help provide for us.

My father, Lucas, after whom I'm named, also worked diligently. After high school, he went to work for a Jewish dry cleaner named Kalman for a number of years, until a close friend suggested he consider teaching dry cleaning at a local high school. At age thirty-seven, my father went to night school to get a bachelor's degree in education and taught during the day. He was tenacious and made a pretty good salary at what he did. He helped my mother pay the bills and made sure there was plenty to eat. But there was a serious problem. His finances and health were often strained by two abusive friends—Jack Daniels and Crown Royal. You see, my father was also an alcoholic. He was sort of a Dr. Jekyll and Mr. Hyde. Throughout the week he was a teacher, but on the weekend he was "the world's worst," the phrase I would often hear him mumble as he staggered into the house and collapsed on the bed. Those were heart-wrenching times for me. Sometimes I didn't think my father would make it through the night. I remember one evening he was so intoxicated that he had to crawl to the bed. I was sure he was going to die. At age ten, I remember hopping out of my bed and tiptoeing to his bedroom to make sure he was still breathing. I did this several times throughout the night, until I eventually tired myself out and drifted off to sleep. I begged him to stop drinking. He promised he would. I was optimistic for a while. But too many broken promises can lead to hopelessness, and even tears. I shed many.

4

If I wasn't smelling alcohol, then it was marijuana. I often watched with wide-eyed curiosity as my older cousins and their friends rolled joints and smoked until their eyes turned bloodshot, while Jimi Hendrix's "Purple Haze" played in the background. As curious as I was about their euphoric state, I never asked to take a drag, nor did they let me. Instead, they practiced tossing me like a ball from one to the other and body-slamming me onto the bed. They said it was a way of toughening me up, of making a man out of me. They claimed the sheltering my mother gave me was going to make me a sissy. In their own way, they were showing me tough love, and their rough-and-tumble nurturing did play a part in my growth into manhood. But I didn't really know what being a man was about until I visited my father's father, Leroy, the man we all knew as Daddy Roy.

My grandfather was a calm, gentle man. He had a farm located in Collierville, just outside the city. And when my father wasn't drinking, my mother would let me go with him to visit my grandfather. Dark-skinned, and standing about five foot eight, Daddy Roy exuded a deep, quiet strength, like the deceptively strong waters of the Tennessee River. He and my grandmother Gladys had four girls and three sons, one stillborn. Every time I saw them together, they always seemed to get along, never arguing. She respected him, and he respected her. I remember him

telling me one time that she did get on his nerves sometimes (I'm sure he got on hers, too), but he said it was
never to the point that he thought about raising his hand
to her, or calling her a bad name.

But it wasn't just my grandmother who respected
Daddy Roy. He also garnered respect from those who
knew him. I know my respect for him was enormous. I
believe if he had frowned at me I probably would have
crumbled. But he never did; he always smiled. I remember during one visit I locked myself in the bathroom. My
grandmother fussed a bit, but Daddy Roy took me outside and simply told me to be more careful. He then patted me on the back, and everything was okay in the
world. He had a way of doing that, of making me feel
special.

I was a short, big-eyed kid, barely weighing a buck-o-
five. Mickey Mouse and I could have been brothers. But
even though I was small, I always wanted to hang with the
big boys. And when it came to work, I tried to show that
I was just as strong as them. Sometimes I would go with
my father to help Daddy Roy during hay-baling season.
One day I decided I was going to do more than just look.
I grabbed a bale of hay that was almost bigger than me. It
took all I had, but I managed to lift it onto the back of the
trailer. My grandfather apparently saw my display of her-
culean prowess and later replied as he stood over several

bales: "Where's that stout boy?" Words can't describe how large I felt at that moment. *I can do anything,* I thought, *if I just put my mind to it.*

I didn't quite understand how my grandfather maintained his peaceful personality, until I was walking outside one day and stumbled across him sitting under a shade tree. His eyes were closed, and he seemed to be mumbling something. I thought he was talking to himself, but as I stood there and listened, I occasionally heard him whisper the name *Jesus.* He was praying.

In the summer of 1995, prostate cancer took him away at age eighty-five. I was twenty-five. Even though he had been sick for a while and the family expected him to go at anytime, his final departure was still tough, especially for me. However, I had a dream a short time after his death that comforted me. I was standing outside my grandparents' house when an angel appeared and told me that my grandfather was going to be all right, but if I wanted to see him again, "You've got to make sure that your life is together," he said. I'd always heard God works in mysterious ways. And when I look back, I truly believe He sent me a surrogate in Henning to help me get my life together.

When I got about five miles outside Covington, I saw the sign that read: Henning, Home of Alex Haley. About a mile down the road that led from the interstate was the

Henning city limits, and a mile from that was another sign pointing in the direction of the museum. As I drove through the small town square and down the street to my destination, the buildings and old homes reminded me of those I'd seen in books about the Old South—the large, frame houses with their columns and spacious porches decorated with flowers and rocking chairs. Then there were the shotgun houses, which signified where the town was once divided between blacks and whites, as was common in most rural southern towns. When I did reach my destination, I was surprised. I expected a building, or a large plantation-style house. But the Haley museum was neither. It was a bluish, bungalow-style home that had been turned into a museum. In a way, I was a little disappointed.

After a few knocks on the back porch screen door, a short, Indian-looking man appeared. "Hi. My name's Fred Montgomery; come on in," he said in a calm, yet clear voice. I could tell he was up in age. But he didn't walk bent over, and his pace wasn't slow but rather quick and short as if he were certain of every direction. I could tell he was of some type of Native American descent. His hair was silvery-gray, and his skin was a bronze color. Large-framed glasses sat on his long, narrow face, and for a moment he sort of resembled a judge, or an old college professor I once knew. When he talked, the peacefulness in his voice hauntingly reminded me of Daddy Roy.

I told the old man my assignment, and he said the best way to learn about the house would be to take a tour. He proceeded to tell me that he was not only the curator of the museum, but the mayor of the town. He said he and Haley were boyhood friends, and later traveled together when Haley was writing the book *Roots*. Based on stories he heard on the front porch of his grandmother's house in Henning, Haley was able to trace his family history back seven generations to his great-great-great-great-grandfather Kunta Kinte. The book eventually won a Pulitzer prize and was turned into an eight-night miniseries that aired in the winter of 1977 and was watched by more than 130 million viewers. I was seven years old at the time and didn't fully understand what I was seeing, but the images and sounds were disturbing nonetheless—people who looked like me tightly packed in the belly of a ship, lying in their own filthy waste for months, mothers wailing over the loss of children they'd never see again, bloody backs.

Haley took the horrific images of the Middle Passage, of slavery, and placed them in the living rooms of households across America. Because of the enormous interest it drew, networks began showing the original series just about every year. Occasionally, the follow-up series— *Roots: The Next Generations*—which was made about two years later, would also be aired. One year when I was much older, I watched the series from beginning to end. I learned values and saw strength and strong moral character that seemed to stick with me, almost as if preparing me for something.

At one point of the tour, Mr. Montgomery pointed to a picture of Haley on the wall right inside the doorway of the museum. He was standing on a dock, looking out across what appeared to be a large body of water. Mr. Montgomery said it was the place Haley believed the first slave ships arrived, and if he was still enough, he told Mr. Montgomery, he could almost hear the wails of the millions of slaves who died during the Middle Passage and see them coming onto the dock in chains, some bloody from being beaten, others near starvation. The curator then pointed to a picture of an old African woman directly on the wall in front of me. Her name was Binter Kinte, the sixth cousin of Kunta Kinte, whose descendants Haley sought in Gambia to find out more about his ancestors. Mr. Montgomery said the woman was still believed to be alive, at age 107. Her piercing eyes seemed to be staring right at me.

As I glanced around the room, I saw to my left different types of Haley memorabilia for sale, including copies of his book *Roots*. To my right was a picture showing all the casts from the two miniseries. Some of them had passed, but many were still alive, like LeVar Burton, who played Kunta, and Maya Angelou, who played his grandmother. As I looked at the cast, I thought about some of the scenes from the miniseries. I remembered marveling at the pride and courage of a young Kunta, who refused to answer to the slave name Toby as he dangled from his wrists and was whipped to near unconsciousness. But I was touched even more by the old black man called Fiddler, played by Louis Gossett Jr. He cradled Kunta in his arms and gently patted his face with water after his limp body was cut down.

"What you care what that white man say," said a teary-eyed Fiddler. "You know who you be: Kunta. That's who you always be. There go' be another day."

I was twenty-four at the time, and I had chosen journalism as my profession. I was so moved by the scene that I used it as the topic of a column. The care shown by that old man for that young man symbolized to me the kind of relationship fathers should share with their sons, grandfathers with their grandsons, and older men in general with any young boy who's being whipped by life's tribulations. It's a kind of encouragement that says, "Stay the course, no matter how tough times get. I've been there, and everything is going to be all right."

Another memorable scene in *Roots: The Next Generations* was when Haley, played by James Earl Jones, discovers the old griot (oral historian) in Gambia, Africa.

"You old African! I found you . . . I found you!" he exclaimed with tears welling up in his eyes.

I took one last look at the cast, then back up at the old African woman before resting my eyes once again on the picture of Haley looking off into the distance. Suddenly, an eerie chill went down my spine. I had a feeling there was a bigger story here than just the museum.

As I followed Mr. Montgomery throughout the house, it was like listening to a tape recorder. As old as he was, he never missed a beat. It was as if someone were whispering every word in his ear. When we got to the living room of the house, I realized a shocking parallel. On the mantel in the room was a picture of a griot, and a young man standing a few steps behind his left shoulder. Mr. Montgomery said the griot was the man who told Haley about his ancestors—the old African he'd found. Haley told him Africans even today believe that when a griot dies it's as if a library has burned to the ground. Haley said the griots symbolize how all human ancestry goes back to some place and some time where there was no writing.

"At one time," Mr. Montgomery said, "the house was visited by leaders from nineteen African countries. One of the leaders was from the Mandinka tribe and identified the old man in the picture as a Mandinka. He tells me this man has nearly five hundred years of tribal history in his head. And this boy never says anything, but follows this man around listening to his stories. When he dies, the boy must take over."

Mr. Montgomery traveled with Haley and listened to the stories he told about his encounters. But not just that; because they were about the same age, Mr. Montgomery was able to give his own perspective about the times in which they both grew up. As I listened to the curator, I realized my position in the room—just a few steps behind him.

I became more and more engrossed in what this old man was saying as the tour continued. He talked about when he was little and how he and other children wanted to go to school, but often couldn't because they had to pick cotton in the hot sun, many times all day. When they did go to school, they tried to learn as much as possible. Mr. Montgomery told me that one time when he was having trouble with his lesson, his mother told him to pray to God, and that the Creator would help him. He did what she said, and after a few months, he was the smartest student in the class. I thought about the importance of today's youngsters hearing his story, especially those who don't want to attend school. But it wasn't just education, there were so many things he said during the tour that could better everybody's life, not just the lives of children. His words of wisdom were like a mental dose of medicine for the painful and uncertain times in which we now live.

After the tour, I knew what the lead of my story

would be. As I drove home, thinking about everything I'd heard, I kept saying to myself, "You've got to tell others about him"—this jewel rich in history and wisdom tucked away in a rural west Tennessee town. It was as if I had discovered a treasure. And for a little while, I sensed the jubilation Haley must have felt when he found the oral historian who unlocked the door to his past. Like him, I couldn't wait to tell what I'd found.

When I got to Memphis, I told some of my family members, and the next day we all went to Henning. They were all moved as I had been, some of them even becoming emotional. Mr. Montgomery and I stayed in touch afterward. On one of my visits home, I stopped by just to say hello. He was done for the day and told me that he was glad I'd come by, that he had something to talk to me about. It was then that he told me Haley had planned to write a book about him but died before doing so. He even pulled out a safe and showed me the audiotapes of Haley's interviews with him. I listened to a couple, and I remember the eeriness I felt hearing Haley's voice.

Mr. Montgomery said writers visiting the museum from as far away as Germany and Canada had inquired about writing a book about him without even knowing Haley had planned one. But he didn't feel comfortable with any of them. They were pushy. However, he said there was something about me. He said I was "young and sort of unassuming," and he liked that. After much prayer, he'd come to the conclusion that he wanted *me* to write about his life. Of course, I was greatly honored, but I didn't know if it was a task I wanted to undertake. I'd never written a book before. Would I do him justice? Would I be able to tell his story in such a way that people would find him as fascinating as I do? I told Mr. Montgomery I'd think about it. As I was leaving the house, I looked once again at the picture of Haley looking off into the distance. For some reason, Haley wanted to revisit the dock in Annapolis, Maryland, after his completion of *Roots*. Maybe it wasn't just a vast ocean he saw, or visions of slave ships and slaves. Maybe he was looking for something.

I contemplated Mr. Montgomery's request for about three weeks, then called him back and told him I would do it. This is his story—a story about a twentieth-century slave who rose to the rank of mayor.

1

TWENTIETH-CENTURY SLAVES

Where justice is denied, where poverty is enforced, where ignorance prevails, and where any one class is made to feel that society is in an organized conspiracy to oppress, rob, and degrade them, neither persons nor property will be safe.
—FREDERICK DOUGLASS

Fred Montgomery was born in Lauderdale County, Tennessee, on November 22, 1916. Back then, cotton was the resource that fueled the county's economy. It furnished the capital that built houses, sent children to school, paid bills, underwrote businesses, and tied black families to the earth as sharecroppers. Black men, women, and children planted, then tilled, and finally harvested each year's crop to share on supposed "halves" with landowners, whom many sharecroppers often called "boss man." The sharecroppers always owed the boss man money for rent, for food, for loans on last year's harvest. With the law in their pockets, landowners kept sharecroppers working on the lands until the debts were paid. Basically, sharecroppers were no more than twentieth-century slaves. Fred and his family were among them.

His father, "Papa," also Fred Montgomery, was a neatly dressed, reddish-colored man who stood close to six feet tall. He didn't say much, and he didn't express himself well. But even though he didn't say it, his family knew he loved them. Papa worked hard, spending all his time trying to make some kind of living. The best he could manage to do was to sharecrop and barber on the side.

Papa's wife, Ionie, Fred's mama, was a petite woman who stood no more than five feet tall and weighed less than a hundred pounds. But her spirit and hot temper made her appear seven feet tall. Nobody messed with Mama.

When Fred was born, Papa sharecropped on Mr. Bob Lewis's farm and made about $150 a year. That wasn't a lot even back then, so sometimes on weekends if he didn't go to the field, he worked at the barbershop in Henning, giving haircuts and shaves for thirty-five cents.

Fred was the seventh of thirteen children, and he and his family lived on the Lewis farm for about five years. As young as he was, Fred was determined to do something to help his family make ends meet. At five, he was thought to be too young to endure the laborious task of picking cotton in the extreme heat from early in the morning to late in the evening. He realized this the first day when he went to the field and didn't get a sack to pick like the older folks. His mama had said he was too small and couldn't pick enough. Well, Fred set out to prove her wrong. He got a bucket and started picking. Each time it got full, he emptied it into a large basket. His activity got the attention of Mr. Lewis, who decided to weigh the basket after he saw it was nearly full.

"Well, I'll be dogged. You lacking three pounds of having a hundred," he said. "I tell you what you do. You go back out there and pick as hard as you can, so you can have a hundred."

A good picking was about two hundred pounds, so Fred considered one hundred admirable. Running back out in the field, energized by Mr. Lewis's challenge, Fred picked as fast as his little hands would let him. By this time they were bloody from cuts caused by the sharp edges between the hulls, a common misfortune cotton pickers came to accept. But that didn't slow him. When he thought he'd reached his mark, he ran back over to Mr.

Lewis. His mother had begun walking over after noticing the spectacle.

"Ionie," Mr. Lewis called.

"Yes, sir," she replied.

"This boy go' be a goodin. He done picked one hundred pounds. Come here, boy, and get this nickel."

Now that was quite a bit of money for a five-year-old. Lye soap couldn't have washed the grin off Fred's face. Ionie also smiled, reluctantly. It wasn't the future she wanted for her children, but her little boy's determination let her know that he wouldn't be afraid to face life's challenges in the future. He would be a survivor, as would his siblings. And Ionie was determined to do her part to help them succeed. Even though she didn't have any schooling, she was full of wisdom. One day she called all her children to her and gave each one a wooden match. She then told the youngest one to try to break it. He did. Then she took about ten of the matches, put them together, and tied a string around them. She told the oldest of the siblings to try to break the bundled matches. When he couldn't, she said to all of them in a sweet, motherly voice: "Together we stand; divided we fall."

It was this belief and their trust in God that sustained most black families, especially under the tough conditions in which they lived. The children often got colds from water leaking through the roof and wetting the bedcovers when it rained. Snowflakes slipped through in the winter. But Ionie did her best to provide warmth by piling quilts and cotton sacks over the children. She'd move from one to the next, asking if they were getting colds or had fevers. If they were congested, on the spot Ionie became Dr. Mama, and with her mouth she sucked the cold from their noses so they could breathe.

Sometimes she put tar on a rag and pinned it around their chests, as well as green leaves from a peach tree. It was an old healing remedy that had been passed down through generations. As the rag and leaves dried, they were supposed to take away the fever. Finally, she knelt at their bedsides and prayed, often fighting tears. All the children lay still, none of them daring to make a move or a sound while she prayed. Her crying let them know she had made contact with God, and they would be well soon. Her faith was a balm for their troubles.

2

KEEPING THE FAITH

Assuredly, I say to you, if you have faith as a
mustard seed, you will say to this mountain,
"Move from here to there," and it will move;
and nothing will be impossible for you.
—MATTHEW 17:20 NKJV

As Fred grew older, he began to ponder this concept of kneeling, closing the eyes, and thanking this person called God for meager things. Who was He anyway? Until he was old enough to know for himself, he just mimicked Mama, Papa, and other people who in distress called to God, who also went by another name he often heard— Jesus Christ. Whoever this fellow was, he came to be like a member of the family when they were sick or were in need of something. Fred kept thinking one day he'd meet him. In case he did, he thought the best way to prepare would be to practice acting like the person believed to be God's best man—the minister.

Standing on a tree stump in 1922, Fred, who was now six, would gather children from the neighborhood around him and proceed to give a so-called "fire-and-brimstone" sermon, often recalling Scriptures he'd heard his mama read from the Bible. If a chicken or dog had died, Fred felt it was his duty to give a funeral.

"We are here today to pay farewell to this dog, who will be missed by us all," Fred would say in a crescendo-ing voice over the shoe box used as a coffin. "He was a good dog, so he's headed to heaven."

Bad dogs were thought to be hell-bound, of course. But Minister Fred prayed for their poor souls anyway. And he expected his congregation to do the same. He was a feisty pastor. If his members didn't shout as he wanted them to, then Fred felt they'd backslid, and he told them they needed to return later to "confess hope in Christ again."

Even though his actions may have seemed comical to some, Fred was actually developing an early relationship with God—one that unbeknownst to him would grow stronger as he got older. But as a child it helped console him and his siblings, especially during tough times when they didn't know where their next meal would come from. He heard Papa and Mama whispering on one such occasion.

"Fred, I ain't complaining, but there's nothing in the house to eat 'cept grease and flour," Ionie said. There was no criticism in her voice, but there was concern.

"Don't worry," Papa said. "I'm going out now and kill us a rabbit or two." His voice lacked passion, but Ionie knew he meant well. She just sighed and smiled.

Papa was a great hunter, a great provider. He was like an African warrior who set out to get food for the tribe, knowing that nourishment of many depended on his day's catch. Fred and his brothers and sisters went to the fields that day and picked cotton till it was nearly dark. Their bellies churned and their mouths watered as they thought about eating rabbit. Off in the distance, they saw Papa returning with his catch. They couldn't quite make out what it was. They were so hungry and expectant they stopped picking cotton and began walking toward their little shack, picking up broken limbs to build up the fire they knew Mama had probably already started. They beat Papa to the house and Mama, as expected, had started the fire. When Papa came inside, he pulled out the meal for the evening—a quail. Disappointment filled their faces.

"Is that all you got?" Ionie asked, trying not to sound too let down.

"This is it," Papa replied.

He had a tone they'd never heard before. There was shame in his voice as he handed his wife the small bird. Ionie didn't say anything else. She knew he was just as disappointed as she was, and that he had done his best to kill a rabbit or something bigger than the quail.

Like a battlefield cook working quickly and efficiently to feed hungry troops, Ionie snatched the feathers off that bird, gutted it, and chopped it into small pieces. Regardless of its size, that quail was going to be supper for fifteen people. She then took a skillet, greased it, and put it on top of the stove, which was now well heated. She poured flour and water into the skillet to make gravy, then added the little pieces of quail. Inside the stove was some corn bread that was almost ready. The aroma from it was so sweet and thick that if the children could have cut into the air they would have had an appetizer.

When the bread was finally done, Ionie rationed out the pieces of meat between herself and Papa. Then she told the children to sit on the floor and she handed them their tin tops, which they used as plates. Each of them got one piece of meat. The rest was gravy with large chunks of corn bread. Before they ate, as always, Papa told all of them to bow their heads and say a prayer of thanks. For some strange reason, no matter how little they had to eat, every time they prayed their bellies were as tight as though they had just eaten a feast. They never went hungry.

Whether it was sitting at the dinner table, kneeling by the side of the bed, or singing in the fields, black families turned to God for strength and comfort. Songs like "Swing Low, Sweet Chariot" and "Soon I Will Be Done" gave them some serenity as they sharecropped, bent over for hours under the sweltering heat of a sun that seemed to have no mercy. The work was backbreaking and degrading. But they were a special people who sought a special strength. With no land, little income and scarcity in other resources, they displayed a faith that seemed to have no measure. They continued to look upward, sending their prayers and melodies to a Creator they truly believed would hear and empower them against their greatest foe—racism.

❋ ❋ ❋

Fred often talks about his faith in God. He tells me about childhood experiences in which God answered his prayer. "I know God will answer a child's prayer," said Fred; "He answered mine."

When I think about my own childhood, I, too, was introduced to God at an early age. My mother would always make sure I said my prayers before going to bed. And when I visited Daddy Roy, he and my grandmother always thanked God for the food. But it was my grandmother's relationship with God, in particular, that intrigued me the most. When she talked about Him, I didn't imagine a deity, but a best friend with whom she conversed every day and who comforted her. As he grew older, Fred also saw God as more of a close friend.

"I never make any kind of decision without first praying about it," he once said. "If when I wake up in the morning I have a good feeling, then I know that's a 'yes' from God. If I feel uncomfortable or uneasy, then that's a 'no.' I trust Him, wholeheartedly."

When I visited my grandmother's church, as well as the one where my mother and her sisters attended, I noticed similar spiritual relationships. No matter how tough their week had been, they seemed to find peace of mind in the words of songs praising God. Oftentimes they would stand with their eyes tightly closed and sway back and forth with their hands raised. Every now and then, tears would seep through, not out of sorrow but rather streams of joyful release. At age nine, I wanted the same relationship they had. I wanted to know this Friend.

One day, my parents and I drove to the country

to visit my grandparents. I had a pony there, and I was looking forward to riding him. However, it had started to rain this particular day, and my father said if it continued I wouldn't be able to ride. I was disappointed because it had been almost a month since I'd visited my grandparents' farm. I wanted it to stop raining. But as I looked at the darkened skies that stretched as far as I could see, my chances of riding seemed slim. Then I remembered something one of my aunts once told me.

"If you want something, ask God for it," she said. "But in asking, you've got to believe that He will answer. You've got to have faith."

I closed my eyes. And in a silent prayer, I asked God for the rain to cease and for the clouds to clear. Suddenly, the rain stopped. And about a minute later, I was amazed at what started to happen. The dark clouds began to disperse, and soon as far I could see was a beautiful blue sky. It didn't rain anymore that day, and I was able to ride my pony.

Some skeptics might think what happened was merely coincidence. But I don't think so. I believe a little boy simply called on God, and He answered a child's prayer.

3

A DIFFERENT COLOR

There is an incredible amount of magic and feistiness in black men that nobody has been able to wipe out. But everybody has tried.
—TONI MORRISON

It wasn't something she enjoyed doing. But when it came to dealing with white folks, Fred's mother made sure her children minded their manners.

"If you're walking in the street and a white person is coming your way, then you get off the street," Ionie would say.

They were also told to use back doors and bathrooms and water fountains labeled "Colored." Black mothers and fathers attempted to instill in their children the laws of the times to keep them from being confronted by whites looking to make trouble. But many times, confrontation was inevitable. Such was the case with a black businessman named Will Palmer.

Will was the wealthiest black man in Henning. He was an inspiration to the blacks, but most of the whites envied him since he had more money than some of them put together. As a young man, he worked at a lumber company for fifty cents a day. The owner of the company was a heavy drinker, and he mismanaged a lot of the money. He got so far behind in his payments that he ended up losing the business. If it hadn't been for Will's hard work in trying to meet the customers' needs, the business probably would have been shut down long before. Ten white businessmen realized the company was very much needed in the area, so they cosigned a loan and bailed the company out. They put Will in charge of the business since he practically ran it anyway. He prospered over the next ten years, making enough money to pay off the debt and own the business himself. Then in 1921 he built his own home. This was definitely a bitter pill for some white people to swallow. They began to harass Will and his family with cross-burnings and death threats. Older blacks believed every time a cross was burned someone was going to die. Fred's mama could see Will's house sitting up on the hill from her window. She often stayed up late at night, praying and peeking through her curtain, hoping that no harm would come to them. Her prayers were soon answered. One day two Ku Klux Klansmen rode up to the house and called for Will to come out. Will, never really showing fear, did so.

"You better not close your eyes in that house," one of the men said. "It's too good a house for a nigger. And if you move in it, we go' burn it down on you and your family."

About that time, the grandson of Dr. D. M. Henning, after whom the town was named, happened to be passing by. He told the Klansmen to leave Will and his family alone. They were, of course, reluctant. But they knew Mr. Henning was a powerful man, and they did as he said. Area blacks rejoiced that such a prestigious white man had spoken up for the Palmers. During the following week, each night as the sun set, a group of about seven to ten women held hands and formed a circle in the front yard of Will's house. They prayed and sang hymns.

"God always got somebody to take care of the poor and the righteous," they joyously testified.

The actions of the businessmen and Mr. Henning showed that there were some whites who believed in fairness. Many others shared the mentality of the Klansmen, threatening blacks and perpetuating demeaning behavior. Some white folks demanded that black men and women call white boys over the age of thirteen "sir." As young as he was, Fred knew this wasn't right. He didn't have to act a certain way with boys his color, so what was so different about the boys a shade or two lighter than him? Nevertheless, he did his best to mind his mother and other elders.

On nice days, Fred and his grandmother would fish together. She told him about her grandparents, who were born slaves and auctioned off like cattle. Though beaten and stripped from their loved ones, she said they trusted in God to see them through the terrible times they faced. She encouraged her little grandson to do the same despite the snarl of racism that glared at him each day.

"I don't know why things happen the way they do," she would say. "But God's going to make it right. There's going to be a better day."

Fred tried to be optimistic. But one day, the glaring got the best of him.

There was a gang of white boys in those days who rode their ponies right through his friends' marble games. The ponies' hooves would kick dust up in their faces and grind the marbles deep into the ground. One day Fred had had enough. When the boys flew by, something in Fred snapped. He jumped to his feet, snatched up the first rock he saw and threw it, hitting one of the boys in the back of the head. The boy screamed, and the boys on the ponies all turned to chase Fred and his friends, who had taken off in different directions. Fred ran as fast as he could all the way home and into the kitchen.

Mama asked, "Why you runnin', boy?"

"Just runnin'," he answered, not daring to look her in the eye. He went to his room and sat there feeling vindicated. But as he thought about what he'd done, he suddenly felt a sense of sadness.

I could've hurt that boy bad, he realized. *Why'd I do that? I've got arms and legs and eyes just like him. The only difference is our skin.*

Fred never told his mama what had happened that day. He never forgot it either. The guilt and anger stayed inside him.

✳ ✳ ✳

Racism is a sickness that shouldn't be inflicted upon anyone. But it's truly sad when children are exposed to it. Fred's introduction to bitter discrimination as a child reminded me of my childhood. And like him, I, too, thought white people were just plain bad. The idea was placed in my head—literally—in the third grade when a white boy hit me in the face with a lunch box and blackened my right eye. I wanted to believe he was just having a bad day. But I later learned he just didn't like black people, a mentality he got from his parents.

My opinion of whites was drawn from older blacks, who would often comment, "You just can't trust them." They were the blacks who had been called "nigger," pushed to the back of the bus, and spit on during lunch-counter sit-ins and other protests in an attempt to gain equal rights. Dr. Harold Taylor was one of those pio-neers. Now an oral surgeon for more than thirty years, he was among a group of people who would gather at a college in Memphis and then walk next door to a pre-dominantly white Presbyterian church and try to enter. When elders and deacons refused to let them in, they knelt in prayer outside the church. Other times they would have marches and sit-ins downtown where they would be cussed at and spat on, a degradation proba-bly worse than being hit. Yet, they were trained not to fight back, but to be nonviolent. I admire their passive-ness because I don't think I could have been as resist-ant. I probably would have ended up in jail for the rest of my life, or dead. That just may have been my fate one day in the summer of 1994 if I'd acted as I felt.

It wasn't quite noon, and I had a taste for breakfast food. Most of the other places near my home had started serving lunch. So I decided to stop at a twenty-four-hour restaurant that I knew would have what I wanted. It was among a chain that had recently come under fire for discrimination on the part of some of its white employees. But I figured not all the restaurants had such problems. I guess you could say I wanted to give them the benefit of the doubt. However, I should have known something when I walked in. The white customer before me was greeted cheerfully as soon as he walked in the door, but there was only silence and stares when I entered. After I sat down, I noticed the two waitresses standing and talking with the cook. They had glanced my way when I was seated. After ignoring me for close to thirty minutes, a customer interrupted them and nodded in my direction. With a look of reluctance, one of the waitresses came over and asked me if I was ready to order in a hurried tone of voice as if she had somewhere to be. I was irate. I wanted to tell her where she could stick the whole menu. Instead I bit my tongue and told her, "No thanks. I think I'll go somewhere else." There was silence and stunned faces as I left.

It was hard for me to believe. Decades after the sit-ins I still was not considered equal enough to be served like everybody else.

Like Fred Montgomery, after having his game of marbles disrupted, the anger stayed with me, also.

4

EDUCATION

If you are planning for a year, sow rice;
if you are planning for a decade, plant trees;
if you are planning for a lifetime, educate people.
—CHINESE PROVERB

When Fred was growing up, education was seen as one of the main ways to beat racism. Some people in slavery times had risked life and limb to learn to read and write. Then, when the Civil War was over, emancipation, like a mighty river, swept through the formerly enslaved South, washing away chains and shackles. Even though faced with ridicule, the newly freed people insisted on book learning. They flocked to hastily established schools founded by churches of almost every denomination.

Fred started school at age six. He and seven of his siblings attended at the same time. Mama and Papa couldn't afford to give them all pencils, so they bought four and broke them in half. But the children didn't care as long as they got a chance to go to school. As young as they were, they knew that school was their main way to bypass the poverty they shook hands with daily. Since their school lasted only four to six months out of the year, they were always so disappointed when the landowner wanted them to miss school and work his fields. Such occurrences were painful for Fred.

One morning, he had his best clothes on to head out to school. Papa came in with a solemn look on his face. Fred knew some bad news was coming.

"Put on your work clothes, son," Papa said. "Mr. Anthony says he needs some extra help today."

Papa knew Fred was hurt, but he didn't say anything. He just left the room. Fred did what he said, but before going to the fields, he went to his mama. Tears in his eyes, he begged her to ask his father to let him go to school the next day. Ionie gently rubbed his face, then put her arms around him and hugged him tight. It was all she could do. As long as they lived on another man's land and worked his fields, neither she nor Papa had any control over their schooling, a situation many sharecroppers faced.

One teacher, Mrs. Carrie Turner, vowed to change that.

"My mission here is to rob the cotton fields of cotton hands," she would say.

Mrs. Turner was unique in that she was a black woman married to a white man, Jim Turner. That allowed her to make such statements without public censure. She loved her people and was determined to do whatever she could to see them progress. Miss Lizzette Murray was no different. A tall, tough woman, Miss Murray wore a tight corset that made her walk as straight as a board. She stood in front of her students like an army general. She was as strict as one too. The fresh-cut switch was always there to remind them of that. Stern as she was, she also loved them and they loved her.

In that little one-room schoolhouse, they felt valued. They felt that they could be somebody. Fred and the other children were taught to respect their teacher; they were told that person is the only one qualified to keep them from being ignorant. If that was the case, Fred and his sister Evergene promised to respect their teachers; they were going to learn as much as their minds could absorb. They fantasized about the jobs they'd get with an education, and what they'd do with the money. Evergene, who was next to the oldest, planned to buy a fancy hat with a ribbon hanging down the back, and bows for her dresses and slippers. Then she pranced around sassily in front of Fred,

41

demonstrating how she would show off her new accessories. Fred, on the other hand, just wanted some pants of his own. He'd been wearing his brothers' hand-me-downs. By the time he got them, there were usually two holes in the knees and two in the butt. But all of that would change after Miss Murray's schooling.

"I'm gonna get a job and make some money," Fred said. "Then I'm go' buy me two brand-new pair of breeches my brothers ain't never had on."

Fred's family moved to Henning in the summer of 1925. They were only a block from the school. Sometimes his mama would walk him. One day, they passed a somewhat large, bluish-colored house with four white columns in the front. Fred thought white people lived there. But then he saw a little black boy playing with a ball in the yard. Could he be the housekeeper's son? The little boy apparently saw Fred staring and asked if he wanted to play. They tossed the ball a couple of times before Ionie told Fred to come on or he'd be late for school. The little boy asked them to wait a minute, then ran in the house. When he came back out, a woman just a little bit bigger than Ionie was with him.

"Hello, my name is Cynthia," she said, "and my grandson Alex wants to know if he can walk to school with you this morning."

Ionie said that would be fine, and they all went on

down the road together. Alex and Fred sat by each other at school and became good friends. As it turned out, Miss Murray was Alex's aunt. His grandfather was Will Palmer, the black businessman who was threatened with cross-burnings after moving into the bungalow-style house where Alex and his grandmother lived. Alex went to live with his grandparents after his mother, Bertha, died. His father, Simon, remarried some years later.

After school, Alex and Fred would often go hunting for hickory nuts or, depending on the time of the year, skinny-dipping. Because he was three years older than Alex, Fred became sort of a big brother to him. And like most big brothers, he got Alex in trouble quite frequently. Grandma Cynthia kept a tight rein on Alex. But one day while she was picking some greens at her sister's house, Fred persuaded Alex to sneak away so they could go skinny-dipping. Fred, who was about eleven at the time, met Alex behind his grandma's house. They took off through a cornfield and across a bridge to a nearby creek. Now, Alex had never been in the water before, so he was hesitant. Fred saw his nervousness and decided to take off his clothes and jump in to show him it was okay.

"Come on, little buddy, it's all right," said Fred, wading in the water. "I'm not going to let anything happen to you."

Alex had taken off his clothes, but he still wouldn't jump. Fred then splashed water up on the bank to try to get Alex wet. When he did, Alex stepped forward and slipped, falling into the water like a bear cub learning to swim for the first time. He splashed around and spit up water for a few seconds before Fred swam over to him. He calmed down once he realized the water wasn't that deep, and a big smile came on his face when he noticed he was actually floating.

"See, I told you I wasn't going to let anything happen to you," Fred said.

But Alex didn't need protection in the water; it was when he got out. As they walked soaking wet down the road leading to Alex's house, waiting on the porch with her hands on her hips and a stare sharper than a butcher knife was Grandma Cynthia.

"Alexander Palmer Haley," she yelled, "you get up here right now."

When she called his whole name, he knew he was in trouble. Fred and the other boys with them knew it also, which is why they scattered like rabbits. Alex's grandmother didn't whip him that day. She waited until she saw him and Fred after church the next Sunday, and then she let them have it. When she finished telling them how disappointed she was in them and how they had broken her trust, they were ashamed to even look at her. Alex later turned to Fred and said: "I kind of wish she had whipped us."

When they weren't skinny-dipping or getting into other mischief, Fred and Alex spent a lot of time writing love letters to little girls, even though they didn't know what in the world they were talking about. They borrowed verses from poetry books that Alex had at his house. The letters would start out, "How are you today? Fine, I hope." Then it would continue, "As sure as the vine grows around the stump, you're my darlin' sugar lump," or, "The river's wide and I can't step it, I love you baby and I just can't help it." Fred noticed that, even though he was younger, Alex was better at writing the letters than he was. The girls seemed to think so also.

Alex's folks had a little money, so he didn't have to worry about sharecropping. But Fred still had to miss many days to help Papa in the field. His family had moved off Mr. Lewis's land, but they still sharecropped for him. The number of days he missed became too many, eventually causing him to fail the third grade. Miss Murray thought he was goofing off and gave him whippings when he continued to do poorly. He just didn't have time to study. By the time he'd finished in the fields, he was too tired to do anything but sleep.

Back then, when you got a whipping at school, you got one at home, too. One day when Fred got home and told his mama the trouble he was having with his lesson, she didn't touch him but rather gave him some advice. She pulled him close to her, kissed his forehead, and said: "God will help you get your lesson." She told him to take his book and put it under his pillow each night before going to bed then pray to God for help. "When you get up the next morning," she said, "the lesson will be in your head." He did what she said. Mama had never been wrong before. She and God evidently had a pretty good relationship because whenever she called on Him when Fred was sick, he got better soon. Fred gave it a try, hopping out of bed in the middle of the night and praying in his cold room.

"God, please help me get my lesson," he would pray earnestly.

One night his papa caught him and asked what he was doing. He said he was asking God to help him better understand his schoolwork. In his usual quiet manner, Papa just turned and left.

Fred kept sending up prayers for a while, never giving up hope that he'd make some type of connection, as Mama always seemed to. Then it happened. After about two weeks, his lessons seemed to be easier, and he started remembering things when called upon at school. After two months, he had caught up with everybody else, and Miss Murray told him he was ready to move up to the fourth grade.

Before graduation, students had to recite a special poem: "If a task is once begun / Never leave it until it's done / Be the labor great or small / Do it well or not at all." Miss Murray wrote the poem on the board and gave each student two weeks to memorize it. Of course, it didn't take Fred that long. He was now personally acquainted with the Person his mother had called on those nights beside his bed. He learned the poem in a day.

❋ ❋ ❋

Fred reminded me of the importance of an education and the invaluableness of teachers, since it is an education that opens doors.

"We were told," he said, "that the teacher was the only one qualified to lead us from ignorance and keep us from being raggedy and poor. We respected them."

When I look back, Hattie Caldwell and Erma Branch—my first- and second-grade teachers—had a lot to do with my success today.

I must admit, I didn't care too much for school at first. It was like greens and spinach, the things I was told I should eat to stay healthy but didn't want. My mother drilled into my head that if I wanted to be somebody one day, I needed an education. Ms. Caldwell reinforced the idea at school. Unlike Fred's

Lizzette Murray, she didn't discipline us with a switch. But then Ms. Caldwell didn't have to be physical. At nearly five-foot-seven, she had a look and a voice that let us know she meant business. However, I'm sure there were times she would have liked to snatch me up. I had this thing about hiding my bad grades. Whenever I made one, I would either trash the assignment or stick it in the back of my folder. I didn't realize it, but Ms. Caldwell saw me throw away some of the assignments. She apparently didn't say anything because she wanted to see how long I'd keep it up. One day when my dad came to get me from school, Ms. Caldwell told him what I'd been doing, and he told my mother when I got home. Needless to say, my mother gave me a severe tongue-lashing. After that, she made sure she saw all my grades. If it was something I didn't understand, she took the time to help me. And if I was confused at school, she told me to ask Ms. Caldwell, to whom my mother had given full martial law rights. They were like the tight defense of a football team. If I ran something past Ms. Caldwell, my mother was there to tackle me.

By the time they finished with me that year, I was ready for Ms. Branch. A slender woman with a mellow voice, Ms. Branch wasn't as stern as Ms. Caldwell, but her attentiveness was the same or better. She took time to make sure each of her students understood their lesson. And we learned early on about great black leaders, such as Sojourner Truth, Madam C. J. Walker, George Washington Carver, and W. E. B. DuBois, just to name a few. She showed us films about different parts of the world that allowed us to look beyond our troubled neighborhoods and dream, just as Miss Murray and Mrs. Carrie Turner lifted Fred and other students in that one-room schoolhouse above the cotton fields.

I never saw Ms. Caldwell or Ms. Branch again. However, my mother informed me some years later that Ms. Branch had died of cancer. My hometown newspaper had done an article about her. Even as the cancer ate away at her body, she continued to go to work. The article mentioned how she made sure all her grades were in order and that other little details were handled up until her last day. She was dedicated. It's because of these two black women that I now have respect for all teachers. In addition to their own families, they have an extended one made up of hundreds of individuals whom they care for as if they were their own. And that's saying a lot considering the meager salaries some of them make, and the fact that they're cussed and even threatened by students who don't appreciate what they're trying to do. It's a long way from the days when youngsters cried to go to school, and teachers were even included in their prayers. But, like Fred, I never forgot those who helped lead me from ignorance.

"God bless Mama and Papa," Fred would pray as a little boy before going to bed. His mother praying next to him would then ask: "What next, boy?"

And Fred would reply: "God bless my teacher."

That goes double for me.

5

THAT SKINNY-LEG GIRL

---
*The meeting of two personalities is like the
contact of two chemical substances:
If there is any reaction, both are transformed.*
—CARL JUNG

As he got older, Fred continued to do well in school, excelling in academics as well as athletics and drama. He was the captain of the boys' basketball team and played the lead role in several plays. He was the darling young gentleman of the community, and nearly every black mother whose daughter was of courting age wanted him. And at age sixteen, his interest for the opposite sex had kicked into high gear. He was long past letter writing, and with his little buddy Alex gone to live with his father and stepmother in Arkansas, he was left alone to explore one of God's sweetest gifts to man.

There were several young women Fred had his eyes on, but Ernestine Bond, a chocolate, skinny-leg girl, was the one who stayed on his mind. He actually saw her for the first time when he was six and she was five, but he didn't pay her any attention because he didn't like girls then. He had a little toy rifle with him, and she wanted to play with it. He wouldn't let her touch it.

Fred never saw her much after that. But one spring evening some years later, when he was about sixteen, he happened upon her standing next to a tree at a church outing. Her neatly fitting skirt-and-blouse outfit, freshly hot-combed hair, and plum-colored lips got Fred's attention. He approached and told her how nice he thought she looked. She blushed, said thank you, and smiled. Fred was hooked. After talking for a while, his stomach began to feel funny, as if, as they say, butterflies were in it. He pushed on.

"By the way," he began, feigning confidence, "may I walk you home from school sometimes?"

"Oh, I don't know," she said.

Butterflies were winging their way through his stomach again.

"I'll have to ask my mother."

Was she just saying that, or did she really intend to do

it? Later that week Fred walked her home and so began their relationship. Most of their times together were fun. There were a lot of things they had in common and some things they didn't. Dancing was one of them.

One night at a party, Ernestine was on the floor dancing up a storm. Fred couldn't dance, so he just stood and watched with increasing jealousy as she twisted and turned with another fellow. Having had just about enough, Fred strutted past Ernestine, went up to Trout Bates, a girl he had known before Ernestine, and planted a big kiss on her lips. About a minute later he felt a hand twirl him around and POW, down he went. When he got up and regained his senses, the left side of his face felt as if it had been hit with a brick. He thought it might have been some guy who liked Trout that had popped him. It turned out to be Ernestine. Boy, she was mad. Embarrassed, Fred went outside to escape the laughter and taunts from his friends. The two eventually made up.

For the most part, Fred and Ernestine had mainly just kissed. But like most teenage boys, Fred became more curious and tried to see if he could get Ernestine to do more than just smooch, to go all the way. She refused. One day, however, out of nowhere, she said she would. But Fred had to promise if he got her pregnant he'd marry her. With his hormones raging, he agreed. They kept it up for about two years. Then it happened.

Ernestine didn't show up for school one day. She sent a note by her sister, Martha, telling Fred that she was pregnant. At that moment, it seemed the whole world had dropped out from under Fred. His teachers and the people in the community had always said he was going to make something of himself. What were they going to say now? Fred, a father? He was still a boy himself. He could do as others had done; leave town and pretend it never happened. But he didn't want to put Ernestine through that— the embarrassment of abandonment. He loved her and he would marry her, if she would have him. It meant dropping out of school.

When the news got to his mama, she wasn't happy at all; neither was Papa. They wanted Fred to get an education, to break the cycle, to be different. This was an old, tired story for them, so they knew what he had to do.

"You not having any schooling is no better than that girl," his mama said. That was her way of telling him that providing for Ernestine and his child, his family, was more important than school. It was a sad truth.

In 1935, at barely nineteen, he had to become a man. The road to manhood was already getting bumpy and financially tough, and Fred wasn't even married yet. He didn't have $3 to pay for a license. Fortunately, he had $3 coming from his janitor's job. His oldest sister, Sally, gave him $2.26. Mr. Light Stokely charged a dollar to drive him and Ernestine to Ripley to get the license. Dilemma: If he had to give him that, he wouldn't have enough to buy the license. Ernestine's mama, Miss Lela, saved the day. She gave them a silver dollar to pay Mr. Stokely and directed them to a cousin who was a jackleg preacher. She said he'd probably marry them for free. After they got the license and Miss Lela signed it because they were too young, they went looking for the preacher.

They found him plowing near his house. When he saw them, he unhitched his mule and motioned for them to follow him. Once inside his home, he took out his hymnal and began to sing. In a solemn voice, he asked Fred and Ernestine to come before him. Then he started praying. When he stopped, he looked down and saw Ernestine grinning.

"I'm going to pray some more, young lady," he said sternly. "This is God's work, and God's business is serious business indeed."

"Ernestine," Fred whispered as softly as he could, "if you don't stop grinning, we'll never get married."

The preacher looked up and asked Miss Lela, who was the only one there on behalf of the young couple, if anyone had anything against their getting married. Ernestine had passed the seriousness test and Miss Lela gave a quick and simple, "No."

After repeating their wedding vows, Fred kissed and

hugged Ernestine. He knew they were facing some tough times. Mama and Papa's absence from the wedding was a clear sign of displeasure. More than that, it signaled a menacing prediction of things to come.

But as he looked into Ernestine's beautiful brown eyes and held her hand, it didn't seem to matter. There was an unexplainable calmness deep in his soul that let him know they'd be all right. If the world were to fall to pieces, they had each other, and a little one on the way—a family. His family.

✳ ✳ ✳

I was never really given the "birds and bees" talk. There were only a few girls I mentioned to my mother and father while in high school, so she probably didn't see any need to lecture me at the time. The only action I got, anyway, was an occasional kiss behind the bleachers during a game, or a smooch or two outside the dance. For me, French kissing was like getting to third base. Yeah, I was slow. But I began to gain a little bit of momentum when I went to college. That's when my mother played Dr. Ruth the best way she knew how.

"Now, you behave yourself," she would say. "There's nothing wrong with having friends. But you don't need to get all involved with some girl right now. Just concentrate on your lesson; that's what's important."

I listened, at least for a while.

In 1988, the second semester of my freshman year, I met a young lady who had apparently taken an interest in me. She smiled every time I saw her, and some mutual friends told me she had been inquiring about me. I played it off. But one day I saw her on campus, and her outfit got my attention. Her snug white sweater and tight-fitting blue jeans accentuated a figure I hadn't noticed before. Suddenly, my hormones kicked into another gear, leaving my mind behind, and I approached her—this time with a smile on my face. We talked for about an hour, then continued our conversation later that night on the phone. We seemed to be hitting it off. After about a week she felt comfortable enough to invite me to her apartment. I agreed to go. Looking back, that was probably mistake number one. After about thirty minutes, we began kissing on her couch. I had graduated to French kissing, and sister-girl was prompting me to hit a home run. I didn't have any condoms, but she said that was okay because she was on the pill. I proceeded to bat. Mistake number two.

The play kept up for the rest of the semester—my dorm room, her apartment, her mother and father's house—until I went home for the summer. One evening, I received a phone call I will never forget. She had called me to see how my summer was going, then she dropped a bomb on me.

"I think I'm pregnant," she said.

There was silence for a few seconds. Then I nervously asked, "Are you sure?"

"I'm late," she said, "and I haven't been able to keep anything on my stomach."

"But I thought you were on the pill."

Again, there was silence, then she replied: "I stopped taking them."

I can't explain how I felt at that moment. It was like being angry and sick at the same time. But what she said next made me feel worse. It was the last thing a wide-eyed, jobless, irresponsible eighteen-year-old wanted to hear.

"If I am, I'm going to keep it," she said.

I'd never felt so helpless. I knew I wasn't ready to be a father. But if she was pregnant, I had to respect her decision, as Fred had respected Ernestine's.

"She (Ernestine) didn't get pregnant by herself,"

Fred said. "I was just as responsible, and now I had to take responsibility. I could have run away like a lot of young men and left her alone. But I wasn't about to do that. We handled the situation together."

Fred's commitment to his responsibilities is an inspiration to me. I'd like to think I would have been as responsible. Fortunately, God was merciful in my case. My girlfriend's pregnancy test came back negative. Apparently, her period was just late that month, and it was a virus that was making her sick.

Needless to say, the incident had a lasting effect on me. Unlike Fred and Ernestine, my girlfriend and I wouldn't have gotten married. But like Fred, I would have been responsible, which would have meant paying child support. However, to avoid any heartache—whether it be financial or otherwise—it's better to wait until marriage to have sex. "It was good advice to wait when I was coming up, and still is," Fred said. "I love Ernestine and my family, but if I was starting over again, I would have waited." He also stressed that being cautious and waiting is the way to avoid getting a sexually transmitted disease that could jeopardize my relationship with the woman I decide to marry.

"How sad, to miss out on a lifetime of love, for temporary pleasure," Fred said. "I was fortunate. You may not be."

6

FIGHTING THE HATRED

Always forgive your enemies;
nothing annoys them so much.
—OSCAR WILDE

Fred and Ernestine spent the early years of their marriage sharecropping on a farm just outside Henning owned by Sam Thum. He was one of those white men caught in a time warp and didn't realize slavery had ended. He was unfair to Ernestine's parents, as well as the three other families who worked on his farm. But because they didn't have anywhere else to go at the time, they had to make do, especially Fred and Ernestine. They had one child,

Charles, and another was on the way. Ernestine's parents insisted they live with them on the farm until they could get on their feet.

Each family was given a few acres to work, just enough to barely get by. If a family was fortunate enough, they would have enough money to buy food to last the duration of the winter months. If not, they would have to take on odd jobs to make ends meet. Every two weeks, the boss man would take up what were called orders. Each family would make out a list of things they needed from the store in town.

If old man Thum approved of what the families wanted, he would rewrite their items on another list and take it to the store. Fred thought the concept was degrading, mainly because if he needed to get something personal, he didn't want some old white man knowing what his wife was wearing under her dress. Then there was Thum's abusive attitude. Fred recalled on one occasion a man wanting to get some dried peaches because his mother-in-law was coming to visit and his wife wanted to make some pies. But Thum told him, "Nigger don't need no dried peaches," and scratched it off the paper.

Thum would never give money, nor would he let the people know exactly how much each item was worth. If he didn't have enough money to pay for everybody's requests, he would borrow from the bank at 7 percent interest. But when it came time to pay for the items on the list, he would charge 25 percent. The high interest affected the workers' crop profit, which meant a lot of people ended up in debt, and the boss man wanted it that way. He didn't care about the well-being of his workers, just his profit. His treatment of Ernestine's parents was proof of his cold character.

Dusty and Miss Lela had been on his farm more than fifteen years. They were hard workers. Dusty was a tall, light-skinned man. Miss Lela was dark, and judging from her strong frame, looked as though she could have put a whipping on most men in her younger day. But they had both gotten old and simply couldn't do what they used to. Dusty was going blind. The boss man called them dead weight because they weren't producing enough and ordered them off his land so a young couple could move into their house.

"I'm go' get me some young niggers to work my farm," Fred overheard him say one day.

Ernestine and Fred couldn't believe it. They knew Thum had his ways, but how could he put out some of his most loyal workers? And in winter on top of that. It was like sticking a dagger in their backs. With the help of Ernestine's brother, Dusty and Miss Lela managed to find a house in Henning.

In 1937, Fred and Ernestine were able to move to

another little vacant house on the farm. From that moment, Fred told Ernestine he was going to start saving to purchase his own house. And he was optimistic. He had dropped out of school. But he was further along than most of the blacks he knew who couldn't even read, let alone spell their own name, like Miss Lela. He accidentally walked in on Ernestine one day trying to teach her.

"See, Mama," she said, writing on a piece of paper, "this is an *L*, an *E*, *L*, and *A* . . . Lela."

Fred fought back the tears. What he saw fueled his determination. He was going to use the little education he had to get the jobs necessary to get off that farm and build a house. It would also be a place for Ernestine's parents, so they wouldn't have to ever worry about being put out again. He told her of his plans, and she began to cry. When he asked what was wrong, Ernestine said in a quivering voice, "I just can't see myself owning a house." Fred took her hand and assured her, "We will; we will."

During the winter months of the fourth year, Fred hustled, taking on any kind of job—shoveling coal, unloading trucks, killing rabbits—to save money for a down payment on a house. That meant making sacrifices in order to live off the profit of that year's harvest. He was able to clear twelve dollars picking cotton. He spent eight dollars on a bed and mattress for the baby, which left them only four dollars to stretch from December to

March. He told Ernestine to hold on to that money. But Ernestine, being young and slightly stubborn, was determined to do what she wanted.

One day when Fred was returning from rabbit hunting, he saw a truck leaving the house. Ernestine met him at the door all excited, eager to show him what she had just gotten—some linoleum to put on the floor, something they really didn't need. In a sweet and unaware voice, she told him it cost only $3.75. Now, the young couple had never had many disagreements. But this time, Ernestine had touched a nerve. For a while, Fred was too mad to say anything. Then he swallowed and asked her for the quarter. That whole night he tossed and turned, wondering how he was going to provide for his pregnant wife and child over the next four months. The burden rested on him, a twenty-one-year-old still struggling to be a man.

That morning he took the quarter to town and bought eight shotgun shells, which he planned to use to kill some rabbits. He could get fifteen cents for each one. That evening he killed seven rabbits and one quail. He left one rabbit at the house to eat and sold the others. He then bought eight more shells for twenty-five cents and shot some more rabbits. On the way back to the house, he ran into Rev. Lionel Nelson, who had been his school principal. Reverend Nelson saw the rabbits and told Fred if he killed forty for him, he would pay him a dime each. He was going to use them for the girls' cooking class at school. The minister suggested Fred get some fellows in the area to help. But Fred reasoned he didn't need any, plus that would cut into his money. The skills he'd learned from Papa about rabbit hunting would pay off. In two and a half days, he delivered to Reverend Nelson forty rabbits. He paid Fred four dollars, which was enough to buy food for him, Ernestine, and the baby. Somehow, they were surviving.

Fred killed enough rabbits that winter to sustain his family until the cotton season. Still, the little money they made from picking and hunting wasn't enough to buy clothes. Fred sucked in his pride and decided to try to borrow fifteen dollars from the boss man to get Ernestine a dress for church and some things for the baby. Borrowing straight cash was unheard of on Thum's farm, since he never gave money. But Fred was willing to take a chance.

It just so happened that one day Ennis Reed, another black man who lived on the farm, was also planning to ask for a loan. The two decided they would go together around noon one Saturday. But instead of waiting on Fred, Ennis, who had a reputation for sneakiness, went and saw Thum early that morning. Fred passed him on his way back and asked what had happened. He told him old Thum had given him what he wanted. Fred perked up and almost ran the rest of the way into town. When he got there, he told Thum why he needed the money. Fred just knew he would sympathize with him because of the baby, but he was wrong. Thum said he wouldn't lend him any money but would take an order as usual. Trying to be humble, Fred told him he preferred the money. But again the old man refused and told him he'd have to do like the other "niggers," which meant giving an order. Thinking he'd given Ennis cash, Fred almost let him know what he could do with his money. Instead, he told him to just keep it and walked away.

As Fred was leaving, he could feel the tears forming in his eyes from anger and the thought of having to tell Ernestine he wouldn't be able to buy her that dress or clothes for the baby. After he'd walked a few feet, he heard Thum call, "Little Red, come on back here." Fred turned around and began walking back, his head slightly down to hide the tears that had seeped through. Thum gave Fred the fifteen dollars. Fred thanked him and left. As he was walking out, he heard Thum mumble, "Niggers always trying to show off." Fred never looked around. The comment fired him up, but he was just glad to have the money. When he got to the store, he saw Ennis with a long piece of paper and no money. Thum had given him an order.

About a year later, in 1938, Ernestine gave birth to another boy who was named Marvin, a cute little fellow with a long head, just like Fred. A third son, named Roy, was born not long after. However, he lived only a month, an actual blessing in this case. He was born with a birth defect that caused him to have spasms all the time and kept him in constant pain. The doctors couldn't do anything to help. When Fred and Ernestine got the news, Fred went outside and prayed.

"Lord, if it's your will, let this child live," he said. "But if it isn't, please put him out of his misery." Roy died about twenty minutes later.

In addition to the money Fred was getting from his odd jobs, the government had started issuing subsidies to farmers. He was now able to put his dream of having a house into motion. A man by the name of William Taylor owned an old hall. He told Fred he would take fifty dollars down payment, and Fred could give him another fifty dollars by that fall. They made the deal, and Fred got a fellow named Bully Green to help him renovate the hall into a four-room house.

Thum was upset that Fred was in the process of buying a house. He had noticed for the past couple of years that he hadn't been coming to him for orders, which meant he was making enough money to take care of all his family's needs. While Fred was picking cotton in the field one day, Thum walked up to him and pointed his finger in his face, so close Fred could smell the molasses he had sopped that morning.

"You makin' too much damn money on my land," he said, turning red as a beet.

Fred replied, "This is your land, and more than half of my profit goes to you. All I'm trying to do is produce a good crop. But if I work the mule too hard, you get mad; if I don't work hard enough, you call me lazy. What do you want me to do, Mr. Thum?"

Thum walked away in silence.

Just as dark, ominous clouds are signs of an imminent storm, Fred knew that that incident in the field was an indication of something very bad to come if he didn't hurry up and move. He almost didn't make it, or, better yet, old man Thum almost didn't.

Fred was tilling land where he had just cut down a bunch of trees. Sometimes the tiller could cut through the stump; however, the stump he hit that day proved to be too tough, and he bent the axle. Thum was out of town at the time, but Fred knew he'd be back sometime that day. He got on one of the farm's mules and went into town to get the axle fixed.

On his way back he ran into Thum, who bitterly questioned why he had been in town on his mule. Fred told him what had happened and that he needed to get the axle fixed. As usual when he got mad, Thum mumbled something under his voice and drove off. Although he couldn't quite understand what Thum said, Fred could make out a few cusswords and the derogatory "nigger." He was heated. *Here I am trying to help the man, and yet I get cussed?*

It was getting dark, so Fred decided to wait till the next day to put on the new axle. He had also decided he wasn't going to put up with that old man's insults anymore. It was time somebody stood up to him. Fred planned to take a shotgun with him to the field when he fixed the axle, and if Thum cussed him, Fred was going to put an end to him.

That morning Fred got up earlier than usual so that Ernestine wouldn't see him get his gun. He had told her what happened before he went to bed. She knew he was angry, and that he hadn't planned to go hunting the next morning. So if she saw him with the gun, she would be worried because she'd know he wouldn't be hunting rabbits, but Thum-hide. As Fred was walking out the door, he spotted a cat chasing one of the chickens. Before he knew it, he had raised his gun and flipped that cat like a pancake. Ernestine heard the shot and woke up. By the time she got to the door, Fred was already in the field, heading to the tiller. Then she saw Thum's truck pass by the house going in Fred's direction. Thum had apparently been watching him. Immediately, Ernestine fell on her knees and began to pray.

When Thum showed up, Fred was just about to

replace the axle. He had hidden the gun in some loose dirt right by the tiller. But to his surprise, Thum didn't utter one cussword. As a matter of fact, he bent down and helped him.

"Here, Little Red, let me give you a hand," he said kindly, almost as if he knew his life depended on his tongue. After they fixed the tiller, not saying anything to each other the entire time, Thum got back in his truck. "Well, Little Red, I guess you're good to go," he leaned out the window and said before driving off.

As Fred watched him leave, he was ashamed. Here he had contemplated killing Thum, and Thum had gotten dirtier than he had fixing the axle. Fred knew he had to leave, soon.

It was no secret that Fred was hotheaded when it came to white folks and their treatment of other blacks. Although he tried to control it, his family, Ernestine in particular, was most familiar with his attitude towards whites. Because he and those close to him had been treated less than humanely for so many years, the dislike he felt toward whites had reached a boiling point—it had turned to hatred.

To help out financially, Ernestine sold candy. Although Fred didn't really want her to, he let her because he realized they could definitely use the money. Once a person reached a certain quota, that individual was entitled to a prize. Ernestine was due one. But when the man for whom she was selling the candy came by to collect his share of the money, he refused to give Ernestine anything because he said she hadn't sold all her candy. However, Ernestine knew she had; the man was just trying to short-change her. He had obviously upset Ernestine, who ran to Fred when she saw him coming up the old dirt road leading from their house.

"That old man don't want to give me my prize," she said, sobbing. "He said I didn't sell everything."

Fred couldn't stand to see Ernestine cry. But more than that, he hated to see her taken advantage of by some old white man. Plus, he knew the truth. He had helped her sell the candy—all of it. He ran inside the house, jumped over the bed, and grabbed his shotgun. By the time he came out, the man was getting in his car to leave. Fred rushed over to the car.

"What the hell is the matter with you?" he yelled, the shotgun at his side. "Why don't you give my wife what she earned?"

"I haven't said I wouldn't give it to her," the man replied, now turning pale.

"She said different," Fred replied.

By this time, Fred had pushed the barrel of the shotgun inside the window and was nudging the man with it.

"Get out and get it—now!" Fred ordered.

The man nervously hopped out of the car and went to his trunk. He pulled out the prize—a package of kitchen utensils—and handed it to Fred.

"Now you get out of here," Fred said.

In his panicky state, the man tapped his gas pedal several times before trying to start the car, flooding it. But Fred was unaware of what had happened. He stuck the shotgun back in the window.

"You can't go, can you?"

Finally, the car started, and down the road it flew, shooting out smoke and kicking up dust. Once again, Fred had let his bitterness get the best of him. But he didn't realize just how deep the hatred ran in his bloodline until a new minister at his church told him a little family history.

One day after service at New Hope C.M.E., Rev. H. C. Walker told Fred he had something he wanted to share with him and asked if he could follow him home. After dinner, the minister told Fred that he had been raised by some Montgomerys in Sardis, Mississippi, in the early 1900s, and that he had known Fred's father's father, Ed Montgomery. Reverend George said at a certain time of the year Fred's grandfather would get drunk and walk to the main road, then flag down vehicles with two or three white men in them and pick a fight. Ed, who was tall and muscular even in his old age, was known in the area for his fistfighting skills. Many times he would get beat up and would have to be carried in the house bloodied. But as if possessed, he kept going back to the road. Reverend George explained why.

When Ed and his younger brothers, Frank and Richard, were in their early and late twenties, their sister went to the store in town. She ended up being kidnapped by three white men and raped by one of them. She managed to escape and ran back home half naked and bleeding. The brothers then went into town. When they found the man who had raped their sister, they killed him. A riot followed, and the three brothers were forced to hide out in an old, run-down house in a wooded area several miles outside of town. They were found after about a month, and when they tried to run, Frank was shot in the back and killed. Fred's grandfather and the other brother managed to escape but vowed never to see each other again for fear they might also be killed. They were never reunited. The bitterness and anger went with Fred's grandfather to his grave.

After the minister left Fred that day, he thought long and hard about what he'd been told. He didn't want to die with anger in his heart like his grandfather. That night before going to bed, he prayed to God to help him be forgiving. He remembered his grandmother Callie telling him that God "wants us to pray for even our enemies, and forgive them." Fred knew it wouldn't be easy. But he trusted God to help him.

✳ ✳ ✳

When I saw *Roots* for the second time and was old enough to fully understand what I was seeing, it stirred up additional feelings of anger. By this time in my life I had experienced incidents of racism, such as the one in the twenty-four-hour restaurant, and I had been exposed to slavery in high school and college history books. There were numerous pictures that disturbed me, but probably the most memorable was the one of a burned body hanging from a tree. I found myself getting angry with the white teachers' attempting to dissect the time period, often showing little sensitivity to the horrific affliction of African-Americans. But it was Fred who helped me change my perspective. Instead of stewing over what had happened to my ancestors, he suggested I look at the strength and determination they possessed to endure their situation. When I thought about their perseverance, I remembered the words to a spiritual I once heard:

I don't feel no ways tired
I come too far from where I started from
Nobody told me that the road would be easy
I don't believe He brought me this far to leave me.

Tirelessness. Relentlessness. Alex Haley's *Roots* probably best depicted the unquenchable spirit of blacks in the character of Kunta Kinte, who despite having half his foot chopped off, continued to run. He wasn't going to let anything stop him from getting his freedom. And then there was the unmitigated courage of the African woman depicted in the character known as Kizzy. After being torn from her parents and worked like an animal, she was raped and forced to breed so that more would come into the world and have to drink from the bitter cup of slavery. I developed a new respect for black women after seeing that. Despite the terrible circumstances that shadowed them daily, some did marry and willingly procreated. However, there were some women back then who spit in the face of procreation. Fred shared such a story with me.

He was giving a tour one day and had reached the part where one of Alex Haley's ancestors, a blacksmith named Tom, was tied to a tree and whipped. A picture of his back showed how the whip had cut into his flesh like butter. As the museum crowd moved on, Fred noticed a young woman crying. It didn't seem unusual at first because many people became emotional during the tour. But this woman began to sob uncontrollably, to the point that Fred asked what was troubling her. After calming down and taking a few deep breaths, the woman said she had learned a few months earlier that her great-great-great grandmother had killed seven of her children. She was about to kill another, but some of her relatives found out what she was doing and confronted her. When asked why she would do such a thing, the woman ripped open her blouse and showed the scars on her back where she had been beaten. She'd also been raped. The woman said she'd rather see her children dead than see them have to endure the same.

"I don't want any of my children to die at the hands of the white man's whip," she said.

Today, slavery has a legacy: racism. Because I detest its principles, it would seem fitting for me to hate its advocates. But Fred taught me that hatred is unhealthy.

"You have to try to forgive and rise above the hatred," he said. "If not, hate will kill you."

According to Fred, those who harbor ill feelings should harness their anger and turn it into a source of motivation to combat racism. He said the torch has been passed from my ancestors to my generation to keep lighting the way along a path that was forbidden to them. That means blacks should attend institutions of higher learning and attain the knowledge necessary to become teachers, judges, and politicians who can make decisions that will promote equality. We should empower younger brothers and sisters to become leaders by taking them back from the streets and letting them know that before their ancestors were slaves, they were kings and queens in Africa, and that they, too, are special—royalty. Fred said this is what the Kunta Kintes, the Harriet Tubmans, and the Marcus Garveys would have wanted. They would be proud.

Granted, there's still a lot of work to be done in the fight against racism, still a long and rugged road to travel. But I'm up for the challenge. Because as I move ever forward, my soul is emblazoned with the fervor of those who went before me. And I don't feel no ways tired.

7

THIS LAND, GOD'S LAND, MY LAND

---

*You can't separate peace from freedom
because no one can be at peace
unless he has his freedom.*
—MALCOLM X

Anytime one man considers killing another man, it's time for somebody to move. Fred had talked about it; now he was really going to do it. Besides, he and Ernestine needed a bigger place. About a year after Roy's death, they had another boy, Fred III.

For a long time Fred did housework on the side for an elderly woman named Ms. Dora Diggs. They became close friends. She was a kind, gentle woman. But a massive stroke had crippled her. And because she was in her eighties, she was finding it more and more difficult to do things around the house, as well as certain personal things for herself. So one day she asked Fred if he and Ernestine would consider living with her, and help pay the back taxes on the house since her illness had caused her to get behind. They said they would. By this time, Bully Green had finished renovating the hall and it was now a four-room house. When Ernestine and Fred moved in with Ms. Diggs, they decided to give the other house to Ernestine's parents. Now, they would never have to worry about anybody putting them out. But best of all, they were finally off Thum's farm. Even though Fred was farming for another man—Mr. Willie Lipscomb—he didn't mind, at least not too much anyway. Mr. Lipscomb wasn't at all like Thum. This new man was fair, and he never cursed. But still, in Fred's eyes, he was a white man.

Ms. Diggs soon died from a second stroke. However, right before her death she deeded the house to Fred and Ernestine. It was 1940, and they finally had their own home. They stayed there for several years, and during that time had six more children all about a year apart. They finally had a girl, Geraldine. She was feisty like her mama, and just as lovely. Then came Henry, Ella, Larry, Derek, and Sheila. Two others were stillborn.

Fred thanked God for giving him his own home. But just as he'd always tried to be somebody, to better his life, he also wanted something better for his family. He felt that God also wanted him to have the best. In order to get it, he had to be totally free, which meant having his own land. As kind as Mr. Lipscomb was, he was still a boss man, and Fred was still working for him. There was also the chance that something could happen to him and his replacement might be someone like Thum, who would make Fred's boys miss school to work in the fields. His boys were now old enough to go to school, and he didn't want anything to get in the way of their education.

At the age of twenty-five, Fred got a job working on the Illinois Central Railroad making $2.22 an hour. He was overlooked at first because of his small stature. He was only about five foot five, but slightly stocky. Most of the other guys who worked on the railroad were robust. But Fred worked hard and proved that he could do just about anything any other man could do. He evidently proved himself because he got the job. He worked diligently until he got the call from Uncle Sam.

World War II had started, and young men were being called to serve. Congress had just passed the Selective

Training and Service Act, which said, "In the selection and training of men under this act, there shall be no discrimination against any person on account of race and color." Many whites didn't think blacks were smart enough, alert enough, or had the moral stamina to fight in a war. But they apparently had overlooked the fact that black soldiers had fought courageously and with distinction in the Revolutionary War, World War I, and just about every other war and conflict ever waged by the United States. The black press, the National Association for the Advancement of Colored People, and the Congress of Racial Equality made sure the usefulness and success of black soldiers didn't go unnoticed. Their constant pressure on the War Department and President Franklin D. Roosevelt's administration for black soldiers to serve equally with white soldiers helped lead to the passage of the act.

Fred was ordered to report to the courthouse in Ripley, where he would leave for basic training. On the day of his departure, he hugged and kissed Ernestine and the children, not knowing whether he would see them again. As he walked toward the door, Ernestine came up behind him and embraced him tightly. When he turned around and saw the tears in her eyes, the sad expression on her face, it was hard for him to let go of her. But he pushed her away gently and told her that he would be fine, that he'd be back. He gave her one last embrace, then turned and walked out the door, Ernestine not letting go of his fingers until the last moment. She and the children watched as he got in his ride to catch the local train to Ripley. They were now left with only his promise to return. He had never broken a promise before. They hoped this wouldn't be the first.

When Fred got to the courthouse, he waited with about fifty other men who listened for their names to be called. Then they reported to a front desk where they were given their exact orders. Fred was listed in what was called Class I, which was to be the first group to go. However, when his name was called and he approached the man at the desk, he found out that he had been deferred indefinitely. Fred was surprised at the news. And Ernestine didn't know what to think when she answered the door and there her husband stood just a few hours later. She and the children joyously hugged him. Fred never got a letter reversing the deferment. He really did want to fight, to show those white folks what he could do. But he liked being back with his family. And, evidently, God had other plans for him.

Fred returned to the cotton fields and the railroad. On the railroad he was at an advantage. He could read. If there was an order and no supervisor around, he explained it to the other men. The same applied to equipment that broke down but had repair instructions available. Fred would read them and tell the men how to fix it. The bosses liked that.

One day Fred noticed two narrow strips of land along the railroad that nobody seemed to be using. He mentioned the section he saw to one of his bosses, who said he would check with the headquarters in Chicago to see if Fred could buy it. When the boss gave Fred the okay, he informed Fred that there was a man letting his cows graze on the land. Fred would have to tell the man to move them to another area. That man, of all people, was Sam Thum. The two met once again, and when they did, Thum, as was to be expected, wasn't too nice.

"Don't you come here tellin' me what I need to do," Thum grumbled, his voice cracking from old age and a bitter heart. "If you touch that land, you gonna get a buzzard picking on you."

In a calm voice, Fred replied, "I've got to die sometime," and turned and walked away.

That next week Fred learned Thum had got together with some other businessmen in town and threatened to sue the railroad if they let Fred buy the land. The railroad later sent Fred a letter saying they couldn't sell it to him, but he could rent it if he wanted. The company also said he would have the first opportunity to buy if they ever sold.

About a month after that, Fred took some money from his savings and bought a mule to plow the land so he could plant cotton. He made a good profit that year. He rented more land and bought three more mules. His sons were now big enough to help him, so his workload became a little lighter. Pretty soon he was averaging nearly twenty bales of cotton at about $120 each. The number soon became thirty, allowing Fred to save quite a bit. He found out that a man by the name of Ed Vaughn had a 37 ½-acre farm he wanted to sell for five thousand dollars and was looking for only one thousand dollars down. When Fred met with the man, he said Fred could pay the rest over ten years. Fred and Ernestine took all the money they made from that year's crop plus some of their savings and made the down payment. Their task now was to pay it off. Fred was determined to do it in two years.

As he had always done, he killed rabbits and did other odd jobs in the wintertime. But this time around he had more vigor. It was almost like he could sense the feelings of his ancestors who toiled on the plantations, working even harder when they knew their chance of freedom was coming—when they wouldn't have to answer to anybody. Death would no longer be their only means of freedom.

Fred plowed from sunrise until around four in the

afternoon, when the boys would get home from school and relieve him. In watching his family work, he realized just how much they shared his dream, especially Ernestine. One day they had taken a break from working in the field to have dinner under a tree. When he got up to continue working, he looked over. She had fallen asleep. He didn't have the heart to wake her. She looked so peaceful and at the same time so beautiful. He went back to the field by himself. As he started plowing, he looked over. Ernestine had awakened and was heading toward him. Staggering slightly, she picked up the hoe and started to work. He told her she could stop if she wanted to. But she insisted on staying and working beside him in the heat, which had to be at least ninety-five degrees.

They had made one two-thousand-dollar payment at the end of the first year and at the end of the second year had enough money to pay the final two thousand dollars. When Fred took the money to Mr. Vaughn, he told him he didn't have to spend all his money now but could pay longer if he wished. Fred kindly refused the offer and gave him the final payment. When he got the receipt that said "Paid," he went back to the field where Ernestine was working and showed it to her.

"Our boys will be able to go to school when they want to and get a good education," he told her. "They won't have to answer to anybody but me and you."

They knelt down on their farm, on their land, and said a prayer of thanks.

In 1949, Fred decided to quit his job on the railroad and spend all his time working on the farm, which had become prosperous. Two years after paying it off, he bought two tractors, purchased a Chevy pickup, owned one hundred acres, rented five hundred acres, and hired some sharecroppers, whom he treated like family. When he had the time, he even did plumbing work for some of the local folks, something he'd learned in his teen years working at the local ice plant. Everything seemed to be going well, and Fred was proud of all his success. But mainly, he finally had his own plot of land, and, for that, he was immensely grateful.

※　※　※

Before he died, my grandfather stressed the importance of owning property. It was a great fulfillment for him to be able to leave land to his children, land they could pass from generation to generation. I remember Fred describing his elation after purchasing his own land.

"All the sweat and tears had paid off," he said. "In so many ways, we were free."

As a teenager I remember dreaming of one day owning some property. My mother's voice often made me wish I could expedite that dream.

"As long as you're in this house, then you'll do as I say," she'd yell when I failed to do something she wanted.

At the time, like many youth, I thought my mother was nagging me. But now that I'm older, I realize she just wanted me to be disciplined, to be assertive, and to do well in school. "If you learn it, they can't take it away from you," she would often tell me. She wanted me to go further than she and my father did. My sisters, Cathy and Stephanie, graduated in the top of their high school classes, went on to get their master's degrees after college, and eventually purchased their own homes. Their success and independence are sources of inspiration for me even today.

Toward the end of high school, I made an extra effort to make my parents proud by graduating with honors. I had always been fascinated with flying and the military, so I endeavored to make the U.S. Air Force Academy my place of higher learning. I received a congressional nomination, but my less-than-perfect eyesight wouldn't let me become a pilot.

Not giving up, I decided to major in aerospace at Middle Tennessee State University. I did well my first semester, but I didn't have the money for private pilot lessons. That's when I realized God apparently had something else in store for me. I decided to pursue my second love, which was writing. I talked to an adviser in the journalism department who turned me on to numerous private scholarships in my field. By the end of my junior year, I had earned enough extra money through the scholarships to get my own apartment off campus. That summer, I got an internship with the *Tennessean,* and the following summer I was able to get one with the *St. Petersburg Times* in Florida. By the time I graduated in 1991, I had enough experience to land an internship with The Associated Press, which turned into a permanent position. I had found my career. It was time to find a permanent home.

Now that I had a stable income, my sister Cathy suggested I stop paying rent and invest in a house. It was time for me to become a homeowner. I selected one from a brochure of homes and discovered that the builder was right around the corner. After a credit check and down payment, the construction began. In a little over six months, I was moving in. I was so excited to have my own place that I kept one of the bricks and shingles left over from the construction, as if I were collecting souvenirs from some faraway ancient site. But probably my greatest joy came in inviting my parents over for the first time. When they saw it, I could tell they were proud of their twenty-three-year-old son, especially my mother. She couldn't stop smiling when she walked inside and saw how neatly the house was decorated. It was hard for her to believe that it belonged to the same child she had to threaten to wash dishes and take out the trash. Her only complaint was a picture of black writers from the Harlem Renaissance hanging above my dining room table. Granted, it could have been somewhere else, but I liked it where it was.

"That picture just doesn't look right there," she said. "If you're going to hang something near that table, it should have flowers in it, or fruit."

Smiling slightly, I said: "Mom, I love you and respect you, but I'm not in your house anymore. I pay the mortgage here."

She shook her head, and then with a smile she herself couldn't hide, replied: "You're right, son. You do."

That evening we sat at the dining room table and

Ernestine in her teens.

Strapping Fred Montgomery
in his early twenties.

Fred and Ernestine many years later, in the seventies.

Fred (front and center) and other men from New Hope CME Church in 1957.

New Hope Church men's choir singing at the opening of the Alex Haley Museum in 1986. Fred is far left.

Fred and Alex Haley.

Fred on a freighter during one of his trips with Alex Haley.

Fred (left) with Alex Haley researcher George Sims (center) and another friend of Alex's in Japan.

Fred eating a Japanese meal.

Fred posing with his aldermen shortly after being sworn in as mayor of Henning, Tennessee—the town's first black mayor.

Fred talking with Don Sundquist during his campaign for governor of Tennessee.

A proud Fred holding two of his great-great grandchildren.

The house
that Alex
bought Fred.

Fred and Ernestine lead family members in prayer.

The Alex Haley museum and house in which Alex grew up.

Alex's Haley's grandfather, who built the house that is now the museum, was one of the first black businessmen in west Tennesee.

Alex standing on a dock in Annapolis, Maryland, the place he believed his ancestors arrived from Africa.

The African griot who holds the knowledge of the village in his head, and the boy who has to learn everything the griot knows.

(LEFT TO RIGHT) Cousin Sis Brooks, Alex's grandma Cynthia, and his aunt Liz, also called Lizzette or Elizabeth. These three women helped nurture Fred and Alex.

Fred and Ernestine in 2003. Below, Fred talking to author Lucas L. Johnson II in 2003.

Daddy Roy, Lucas's grandfather, holding Lucas.

laughed and talked a long time, in the company of Langston Hughes, W. E. B. DuBois, and a bunch of other prominent black folk—in my house. Thanks to the perseverance and diligence of men like Fred, it's easier for men like me to achieve the dream of owning a home.

8

WHY, LORD?

Although the world is full of suffering,
it is also full of the overcoming of it.
—HELEN KELLER

Sunday evenings in the early summer were Fred's favorite time to relax. Sometimes after church he'd come home and raise the windows in the house or sit on the porch, listen to the radio, and enjoy an occasional cool breeze as the sun set. It allowed him to reflect on his life, his family, on everything he had gained in his nearly fifty years of life. On this particular evening in 1963 one of his favorite songs was playing on a Christian station: "Jesus, Keep Me Near the Cross." He listened intently with his eyes closed, meditating on the words, almost as if God were preparing him for something. Then, suddenly, the phone rang. And he got the news.

"Henry has drowned!" yelled a sobbing voice on the other end.

Henry was the sixth child, a smart, energetic young man whom Fred had planned to send to trade school to become a master plumber. But how was he to know that plan would be cut short at nearly eighteen? Fred stood there, holding the phone in disbelief. Then the caller, family friend Geraldine Harding, told him where it happened, and that he needed to get there. It was Keller Lake, about a mile outside of town. On his way Fred decided to go by and get Ernestine, who was at a missionary meeting at church. He kept thinking to himself, *How am I going to tell her? God, please help me.* When he arrived she was coming out of the church, smiling and talking with other members as if she didn't have a care in the world. She knew Fred like a book, however, and the look on his face showed what his heart felt. Taking a deep breath, he told her what had happened, and she started screaming and running. He chased her down and pulled her back to the car where she passed out. He took her home, and a few church members came along to help watch her.

When Fred drove up to the lake, there were a lot of people standing around. The police told him they still hadn't found Henry's body and that they were about to drag the lake again. Fred heard the words, but everything seemed to have lost meaning. He just stood there in that one spot, staring at the watery grave that supposedly contained his son. The rescue workers were using giant hooks to drag the lake. Then one of the rescuers indicated that the hooks had grabbed onto something. Within a matter of minutes, a limp body was brought to the top of the water. It was Henry. As Fred watched them carry his body to the ambulance, he couldn't believe his son was dead. He looked as if he were only sleeping and as though he'd respond if Fred just called his name, as he had so many times before in the mornings, in the evenings, and at night. No voice would be heard this time. Even worse, Fred would never be able to tell him what he always felt but was never able to say. That he loved him.

The ambulance pulled away with Henry's body, and people began to leave. Fred just stood there in a daze. After a while, a close friend, Neely Johnson, put her arm around him and guided him away. When he got home, the doctor had just given Ernestine a shot to relax her nerves.

Henry's funeral was about three days later. Fred managed to get Ernestine up that morning, and some of her friends came by to help her get ready. She was in a complete stupor. On the way to the funeral, Fred would hear her say every so often, "Henry is gone; my Henry is gone," then she'd weep, every tear cutting into his heart. But Fred knew he had to be strong for her. As they walked into the packed church, Ernestine turned to the people sitting at the ends of the pews as she passed and somberly expressed her pain: "You just don't know; you just don't know."

Nobody could really know the pain Fred's family felt. It was a while before the rest of the kids were back to normal. Ernestine stayed in bed for almost a month following the burial. Fred had to be strong for everybody. To try to ease his mind, he threw himself into his job. And when that wasn't enough, he got involved in local politics, running for—and winning—a seat as an alderman. It felt good to talk for his neighbors and get things done. Yes, things were a little better. But he couldn't help but think, *Lord, if something like this happens to one of mine again, I don't know what I'll do.*

Sometimes life can be so cruel. Sometimes it seems God isn't there. But He is, and He never gives anyone more than he or she can bear without also providing the strength to make it through. It took another test for Fred to see that God is never far away.

It was a bitterly cold day in January of 1978. But weather conditions didn't really matter much when it came to hunting. It was something that Fred, his son Fred III, and some other fellows did all the time, and they would do it in almost any kind of weather.

They had just finished rabbit hunting on Shoaf Island, about twenty miles west of Henning near the Mississippi River, and were in their boat heading back down the river.

The water was rough, and it was so cold that splashes froze instantly and fell like rock fragments. Big chunks of ice the size of couches floated around the five of them—Fred III, Fred and his son-in-law, Robert Lee Mosby, and two other men. They also had five hunting dogs. The water seemed to get rougher as they floated on down. Then, suddenly, a strong current caused the boat to shift, throwing the men to one side. It then capsized, forcing all of them into the water. One of the dogs immediately jumped on Fred's back and pulled off his life preserver. His son pushed an empty gas barrel that had fallen from the boat towards him to hold on to. In a matter of minutes, they felt the frigidness of the water, which was in the teens. Fred's bottom half was starting to go numb. His son and son-in-law said they were going to swim to the bank and get help. They didn't have but a few feet to go. But within minutes, Fred heard the screams of a man calling for help. Then a deathly silence followed. He looked around and saw the dogs turned on their backs, going under. Robert had managed to grab onto the side of the boat, which had resurfaced bottom-side up.

They were now alone, in the cold and the darkness. As the chunks of ice bounced off their bodies, they began to drift in and out of consciousness. Fred's confidence failing him, he knew death was now a strong possibility. But he wasn't afraid. As he had always done, his concern was for Ernestine. He just wanted God to strengthen her, that she might be able to handle the loss. His thoughts were suddenly interrupted by scratching, then a gurgling sound. Again, there was silence. With as much breath as he could muster, Fred called out: "Robert Lee! Robert Lee!" When he got no answer, he knew his son-in-law was dead.

Pretty soon, Fred started to black out completely. But before he did, he saw what looked like a boat approaching with two men on board, both wearing black hoods. That's the last thing he remembered.

He woke up in the hospital. The doctor standing over him was apologizing because he'd had to slap Fred a few times to help him regain consciousness. He told him he was lucky to be alive. He had been in the water almost an hour and was comatose for nearly three hours. The nurse gave him some medicine, and he went back to sleep. He awoke to find another white man standing over him. He was a somewhat tall fellow, with an eerily calm look about his face. Fred was a little startled at first, then the man told him who he was and what he had done—and a chill went down Fred's spine. He said he was one of the two men Fred saw before he blacked out. They had pulled him out of the river. But the thing that stuck with Fred the most was that the man was a preacher. *God's best man saved my life,* he thought.

Growing up, Fred was always taught that the minister is favored by God, to guide the flock. The minister, who was steering the boat, said he hadn't planned to come in

Fred's direction, but something compelled him to change his course. When he found Fred, he was as stiff as a board. His glasses were frozen to his ears and the minister was afraid to remove them because they might pull his ears off. He told Fred he ran to some of the houses along the river to get help, collecting blankets, sheets, anything people could give to put around Fred and Charles Halliburton, the other man who survived. With the residents' help, they managed to take the two men back to their trucks on the bank near the river and turn on the heat in the vehicles until the paramedics arrived. Just when Fred was about to ask him if he knew anything about the others, one of Fred's daughters, Sheila, walked in. He first asked her about his son. She said he was okay, then she broke down into tears. Fred knew then he didn't make it. He later found out that Charles's brother, Larry, also had perished.

When Fred got home from the hospital, Sheila had made up a bed downstairs for him to sleep. But he wanted to go upstairs. He went into one of the rooms and fell on his knees with both hands in the air, tears running down his face. He wanted to ask, "Why, Lord? Where do I go from here?" but he was too choked up to produce a sound. He just knelt there, humming the song "Precious Lord, Take My Hand," trying to release the pain through the streams of tears. The ones he never cried for Henry were now joined with those for Fred.

Following the funerals, life was painful. Fred III and Robert were the backbone of the family plumbing business. They drove two of the three trucks Fred operated. He felt as though both his arms had been cut off. Some days he didn't feel like doing anything. And when he did, he struggled. Gloom seemed to be all around him, literally. There were times he'd look up and a mist would be following him wherever he went. One day, he decided he just couldn't take it anymore.

He got in his pickup and headed for the bridge leading out of town. Once he got on it, he pushed the accelerator to the floor and tried to drive over the side, but the steering wheel wouldn't turn. However, after he'd made it across, the wheel miraculously unlocked. Possibly, it was just a fluke occurrence. It wouldn't happen again. He'd make sure of it.

After tucking a copy of his will under his pillow that night, Fred slipped outside quietly so Ernestine wouldn't hear him. This time he got behind the wheel of his car and again headed for the outskirts of town. When he got to the railroad tracks, he glanced at his watch. It was around eight-thirty. He drove the car right up onto the rails, put it in park, and turned off the engine. Now all he had to do was wait. The train would pull through at nine o'clock. He'd never known it to be late. Soon he'd hear the whistle in the distance, then he'd see the locomotive bearing down on him and it would be over.

He sat in the driver's seat, staring down the tracks, listening for the nine o'clock whistle. Nine o'clock came and went. Nine-fifteen. You could practically set your watch by that train, and yet it had not come through. By nine-thirty he began to worry that someone might see his car on the tracks and get suspicious. He decided to move it, then go back and sit on the tracks. While he was parking the car behind some bushes, there was a loud whistle and the train zoomed by.

There's another one due at ten, he thought. *I can catch that one; it won't be late.*

So at 9:45, he sat down on a railroad tie. Ten o'clock came and went, but the train did not. He finally gave up at ten-thirty and headed back to his car. Just then, he heard a whistle as a train whizzed by. He couldn't believe it. He went back home, and there he again fell on his knees and cried, "Why, Lord? As old as I am, you let me live, but didn't spare those young men. I don't understand. Why?"

He prayed long and hard, but he could not come up with a reason. He cried himself to sleep, his will still under his pillow.

The next morning, Fred awoke to see a sun he hadn't expected to see the day before. Still somewhat dazed and heavy-laden from crying nearly all night, he slowly dressed to go into town. Once there, the strangest thing happened. Nearly every person he encountered had something nice to say about his son, or some other words of comfort.

Everyone, even the grown white men he'd always thought hated him because he was black. But now, he realized all those white people didn't hate because they, too, had experienced a painful loss at one time or another. That's why they were able to cry for him, and with him. As they did, their tears seemed to flood Fred's heart and soul, cleansing him of his grief, as well as the animosity he'd felt toward whites for so many years. He had lost several loved ones, but now he had an extended family of numerous brothers and sisters.

"God made us all, and we're all his children," he realized.

Fred also believed he'd find out why God had kept him alive. Like the faith he saw his mother have when he was a child, he had to "be still and know" that God would give him an answer.

"God does things for a reason, one that we will understand by and by. Until then, we must continue to put our trust in Him, because He will sustain us," Fred explains.

❋   ❋   ❋

During one of my visits to Henning, I stood on the railroad tracks where Fred had attempted to take his life. I faced the direction the train was supposed to have come from that night and tried to imagine it coming at me, its whistle blaring, and then finally tons of steel crashing into my body. It was unfathomable. I couldn't imagine committing suicide.

My mother and grandmother would always say, "God will never put more on you than you can bear." However, a battle between good and evil has been waged since the beginning of time. And the latter wants you to believe that life's negative occurrences can be too much, forcing one to turn to a means of escape such as drugs, alcohol, or the ultimate false sense of freedom—suicide. Fred tried it as a way of escape.

"At the time, I couldn't see the pain ending. It didn't seem like it was ever going to ease off," said Fred, referring to life after losing another son and his son-in-law. "I couldn't sleep. It was like a recurring nightmare, and I just didn't want to endure it any longer."

But after God snatched him from death, and gave him a new lease on life, he now realizes that "God was there all the time, and I should have kept trusting in Him to take away the pain, because He would have eventually."

I know the feeling all too well of waiting for the pain to go away, especially in the case of a loved one who's suffering.

Daddy Roy had gone to the doctor after having problems seeing. Doctors discovered cataracts in both eyes. But before operating, they ran other tests and drew blood. My grandfather was always leery of doctors. He would say: "They're like mechanics; you take your car to them for one thing, and they find something else wrong."

In his case, they found a big wrong. Blood was discovered in his urine. After running further tests, he was diagnosed with prostate cancer. It was the last thing any of us expected. At first, like many cancer patients, everything was fine. He continued to get up before dawn to farm—feeding his cows, horses, and pigs, and tilling the land on his tractor until sunset. Then, gradually, things began to change. His back started to ache, and each day the pain seemed to get worse. Then it was his appetite. He began losing weight and was frequently nauseous. He loved my grandmother's homemade biscuits. She made them for breakfast, lunch, and dinner. But my grandfather got to the point where he would barely touch them. We didn't want to face it, but the cancer was spreading. And it did, rapidly zapping his livelihood and energy before our very eyes. It all seemed so unfair. This was a man who had always tried to do good, who loved his family and others. In their younger days, he and my grandmother owned a small store. When times were tough, they would let some customers, including a few whites, have items on credit.

Daddy Roy enjoyed it when everyone would get together and sit around the table at his house, eating and laughing. Visitors were always welcome to join the family at meals. We tried to continue the tradition during his sickness, but it just wasn't the same. It was tough looking at his empty chair, knowing he was in the back room, fighting for his life.

I saw him a few weeks before his death. My mother had called me and told me he probably didn't have much time, and I needed to come see him. When I got there, my aunts and cousins greeted me with hugs and smiles. But that lasted only a moment, and their expressions soon faded to worry. It was tough for all of us because my grandfather was such a hard worker, a fighter. I remember stories about how, at age twelve, he drove a log wagon of eight mules and horses to help his mother take care of his three other siblings. He maintained that same work ethic the rest of his life, until cancer forced him down.

As I walked down the hallway leading to his bedroom, it seemed longer than usual, as if I were moving in slow motion. But no matter how much time I took, I don't think anything could have prepared me for what I saw. This wasn't the same man I'd seen about six months earlier. The man before me was much darker, and his skin was wrinkly and loose, as if it had been draped over a skeleton. The cancer had spread to his chest area, filling his lungs with fluid, which hampered his breathing. Some of my relatives took turns helping him cough up phlegm to ease the congestion. I wanted to cry. Dazed, he looked at me, but I don't think he recognized me. I stepped closer and leaned over and kissed him on the forehead. That was the last time I saw him. He died about two weeks later.

As a result of his experience, Fred says he has a stronger relationship with God, whom he depends on to do everything. When I listen to him talk about his best Friend with joy and sincerity, I'm reminded once again of my grandmother Gladys, whose belief in God is so strong that she asks him what clothes to wear before she leaves the house. I used to laugh at that, but I don't anymore.

"I can do all things through Christ who strengthens me," she often says, quoting Philippians 4:13, one of her favorite scriptures.

Undoubtedly, her faith and love played a big role in the salvation of my grandfather.

9

NEW LEASE ON LIFE

---

*Courage and perseverance have a
magical talisman, before which difficulties
disappear and obstacles vanish into air.*
—JOHN QUINCY ADAMS

About a decade had passed since Fred's brush with death.
His close call, as well as the kindness shown by so many
white people, gave him a new outlook on life. He had
made a lot of long-lasting friendships while in the plumbing business. Many people remembered the kindness he
showed when he did work for them. It paid off by helping
him win the seat of alderman. While in that position, he
spearheaded the effort to get a $240,000 grant to renovate

Bates Street and what was called the Colored Lane, the poor section of Henning where most of the blacks lived. The money was used to put in a sewer line, install a new gas line, and put a fire hydrant in the area. The grant won favor with the people, and set Fred up for his next big political move.

After writing the book *Roots,* Alex Haley became a household name. That meant automatic attention for his hometown of Henning. He talked the state of Tennessee into turning his boyhood home into a national museum. Alex asked Fred to be the curator. They remained close even after their boyhood days. They had always been more like brothers than friends. Alex often invited Fred on some of the long trips he took to write. In 1988, he wrote the museum board and asked permission for Fred to sail with him to Japan. At one point during the trip, a conversation was struck up about the upcoming 1988 mayoral election in Henning. There were several prospects, and Alex told Fred later that evening that he thought he should be the one to run. Fred said he had considered the idea, but wasn't sure. However, the issue of running weighed heavily on his mind the next ten days. He prayed, with the hope that God would give him an answer. He soon got it.

The first thing he did when he got back from the trip was meet with some of the blacks who were considering running. That was the Bates family. He met with three of them—Robert, John L., and Matt—at their house to discuss the need for a black mayor. They all declined and said since Fred had been on the board of aldermen the longest, they'd support him. Their slogan was "Together We Stand."

Fred then went around to all the black churches and let them know that he was running. He was surprised to discover how unsupportive some of his own people were. A lot of them were afraid, saying the town wasn't ready for a black mayor. Others simply doubted his ability, saying at age seventy-one he was too old to run. Even though he'd been successful politically as alderman, many thought with little education he wouldn't succeed as mayor. Then a huge dagger was thrown from the other side. Fred got word that this town didn't need a "nigger" mayor. But he wasn't about to back down. The remark just made him even more determined.

Fred went beyond the churches, going to gambling dens and even Chocolate City, a little juke joint outside of town where blacks went to drink and dance. His supporters even had some of their meetings there. The more he went around and talked about the things he would do for the town, the importance of having registered black voters and the timeliness of electing a black mayor, the more it seemed people started to listen to him and change their minds. They were starting to believe. He found out that many who had sworn they'd never vote were registering.

Fred continued to make pitches on his plumbing rounds. He was the town's first black master plumber. When he went to the houses of old white widows, Ernestine would go with him because it was still dangerous for a black man to be seen coming out of a white woman's house by himself, no matter how old he was. Some women would call late at night, early in the morning, whenever they had a problem. Ernestine didn't mind accompanying Fred because she knew it was for his own good. Her job was to talk to the women while Fred worked. One of his favorite clients was Miss Agnes Pipkin, a jovial little old white lady who always wore a smile as bright as the sun. She had known Fred most of his life and always trusted him. When he was younger, he was the first black person the Pipkins allowed to work the cash register in their store, Henning Supply, the largest in the town at the time. One day, after doing some plumbing work for Miss Pipkin, she told him before he left her house: "Fred, I've been knowing you a lifetime, and you just seem to be different. Would you promise me something?"

"Yes, ma'am," Fred said.

"Will you promise me that if I vote for you and get you elected, you won't get uppity and stop coming to see about me like you been?"

"Miss Pipkin, I don' think I'll ever forget about you," Fred replied, laughing.

Miss Pipkin was one among many white people who promised Fred their vote. Some, however, said they would vote for him but asked that he not tell anybody. He promised he wouldn't. Heck, he didn't care if they were two-faced or not, as long as he got their vote. The ballot box didn't discriminate.

Soon it was voting day, and Fred and his campaign rejoiced. Black people from the Colored Lane flooded the polls. There were people like Jessie Lake, who rolled down in her wheelchair to vote, and Richard Pete, a blind man who had quit voting and swore he'd never vote again. Then there was an eighty-eight-year-old white lady named Mrs. Virginia Tuholski, considered the matriarch of Henning. Her maid helped her to the voting booth, and she told the local newspaper she was voting for Fred because "he's honest." His heart swelled from all the support. Before the voting booths closed, Fred ran into his opponents, two white men. He told them that after much prayer, God had revealed to him that he was going to be the next mayor of Henning. They both laughed. But Fred had the last laugh. The final tally showed he had more votes than both of them put together.

During the time Fred was elected, the mayor of a small town like Henning also had to serve as judge. This was a challenge for Fred. Not so much because of the extra duty, but because of problems with his own people, as well as whites. Blacks who knew him thought they should get by with a warning, and some whites simply didn't think an old black man should be telling them what to do. But as he'd always done, Fred met the controversy head-on.

In one case, a teenage boy speeding through Henning at 80 mph was chased by police until he ran off the road into a cotton field and got stuck. Police arrested the boy and took him before Judge Montgomery. When some of the town folk got word that the boy had been arrested, they were shocked. They knew his father, a mean, burly white man, to be a troublemaker, and they felt Fred would be intimidated by him. But they thought wrong. When the man came to court with his son, he was huffing and puffing angrily. But Fred told him he should be thankful.

"Wouldn't you rather come down here and pay a fine, than go to a funeral?" he asked.

"Well, I don't really want to do either one of them," the man said.

"Suppose I would have let him go," Fred continued. "He might have killed himself or someone else before he got to where he was going."

The man reluctantly paid the fine.

Fred got all kinds of threats. One person even threatened to burn down his home. But Fred didn't run and hide. He continued to walk the streets of his town like everybody else.

"If they want to burn my house down, let them," he said. "I'll build a new one."

Fred had a reason to be beyond fear. He was seventy-one years old, and God had spared his life several times. No man was going to decide when he should leave this earth. Only God would be the judge of that.

❋   ❋   ❋

After all Fred had been through, in the end, God showed him that He's in control. Fred simply had to have faith and trust Him, as Fred's mother, Ionie, had done, and other blacks who called God's name when in despair. Fred didn't run for mayor until he was assured in his heart that God wanted him to. Likewise, most of the men in my family saw their mothers, aunts, and grandmothers fall on their knees in prayer when they needed guidance. That would explain why nine of them—my father and eight others—who battled substance abuse knew who to turn to and eventually found peace of mind when they stopped looking down on themselves, looked up, and let Go(d).

In the case of my father, however, I must admit, it was weird at first. Around my second year in college, he all of a sudden stopped drinking. And he started acting like the fathers I'd read about in books or seen some of my friends have. His assistance was now constant. When I needed transportation, he helped me get my first car. He seemed like a new man—healthier, livelier. He said he had been sober for a while. But at times I was skeptical. I wanted to accept this new person, but I was afraid I'd be hit once again with another broken promise. I'd had too many of those as a child. However, as the year went on, and I visited home, I encountered the same sober man each time. Maybe he had changed. We finally talked about it, and he explained what had happened. He mentioned all the times he'd broken his promises to me about drinking. He said the disappointed look on my face was heartbreaking. He felt trapped. He wouldn't ever be able to stop because he was sick.

At that point, he contemplated taking a gun and blowing his brains out. But just as he was about to reach for the gun, he got down on his knees and pleaded with God to remove his taste for alcohol, to "please wipe it from my mouth." By that evening, he had no desire to slip out of the house and go to the liquor store. It was Saturday. Sunday, no taste.

Monday, no taste. Weeks went by, and still no urge for even a cooler. It's been more than fifteen years, and my father is still sober. His prayer was answered. Likewise, God also heard the prayers of the other men in my family once addicted to everything from heroin to cocaine. They all are now sober. The youngest of them, however, is serving the remainder of a fifteen-year prison sentence. He said being incarcerated has disciplined him and helped turn his life around. But when I think about how he ended up where he is, I feel partly responsible.

My cousin Harold was exposed to marijuana as an infant. His father was a supplier of it, and he and Harold's mother were big-time users. When Harold and I were both nine years old, we watched our older cousins get high. They would often let Harold take puffs just to see how he would react, but they would never let me smoke. They felt Harold was used to it because he had inhaled it since birth. But they didn't let me because they thought I was the smarter one, that I was going to "be somebody," and they didn't want to mess that up. It was as though my and Harold's fates depended on their misconstrued judgments. Even though I was as young as Harold, a guilty feeling remained with me most of my life when I thought about how I just sat there and said nothing to try to dissuade him. I just watched him through the smoke that was growing between us, dividing us, a symbol of the paths we would later take in life.

As he got older, Harold became more and more locked into the cycle of drug usage. His folks were no help. They both became addicted to crack cocaine, which eventually caused them to break up. His mother skipped town and left Harold with his father. At age sixteen, Harold became a father himself. But because he was in and out of jail, he hardly ever saw the child, named Devon. Harold's father tried to make up for lost time by attempting to raise the little boy and enrolling him in school when he found out he wasn't going. However, the grandfather's addiction got the best of him, and he also ended up in jail. He and Harold served six months together. Can you imagine? Doing work detail in the cafeteria and watching your father come down the line each day.

Now Devon really had nobody. He was sent back to his mother, who at the time was already taking care of five other children by herself. And his father was still battling his own demons. Harold twice tried to overdose on pills, but his attempts failed. The family tried to reach out to Harold over the years, but he slapped everybody's hands. After burglarizing the homes of two of his aunts, he was involved in a botched drug deal that left him with a charge of second-degree murder. He had now graduated from jail to prison, and it would be his home for a while. The last time I went to see him, he looked good. He said he'd asked God to forgive him, and that he was continuing to pray and read his Bible. I told him to stay strong. We both pondered why God had spared him from the attempted suicides and other brushes with death. Just as God had a reason for sparing Fred, he also had a purpose for Harold, if nothing but to be a testimony, like our cousin Anderson.

After going straight, Anderson had to appear before one of Memphis, Tennessee's toughest judges for a violation of probation that occurred during his cocaine addiction. He faced jail time. But after Judge Ann Pugh read an article I'd written in *Essence* magazine about Anderson's recovery and all the positive things he'd been doing, she was moved to tears and dropped the charge against him. (See the complete article in the Appendix.) When my cousin called me at work and told me what had happened, I was in disbelief and jokingly told him: "You've been smoking again, haven't you?" After he provided more details, my doubt started to change. He said there were others in the courtroom that day also crying, and that he had an eerie feeling, as if "someone or something unseen was also there." When I hung up the phone, the reporter in me had to know more. So I looked up the number for the Shelby County General Sessions Criminal Court to reach Judge Pugh. When I called, I asked her to send me a letter detailing how she felt that day. She told me her schedule had been "out of control," but that she would send me something. I expected maybe a page. I got three. This is some of what she wrote:

> It is really difficult to express what I felt on that last day when Anderson Jackson Jr. appeared before me for final adjudication of his violation of probation charge. Quite honestly, I don't know how to describe my feelings. I know that my reaction was something very out of the ordinary for me. I have been a judge for fifteen years, and during that time I have seen many

failures and ruined lives, but I have also seen several successful turnarounds and positive steps. Thus I cannot really explain why your article about Anderson touched my emotional chords so dramatically. Perhaps it was because I had experienced a long period of time with nothing but bad news, a long dry spell of feeling "What good am I doing here," a long time of no positive reinforcement. But I started reading your article about Anderson silently, at first, and then just started reading it aloud—and over the microphone. Everyone in the courtroom could hear.

The more I read, the more emotional I became—to the point that I could not read at all for the tears that were freely and uncontrollably flowing from my eyes. There was a time of total silence—then I continued reading, my voice quivering. I think the article brought out the hopelessness, the anguish, the total frustration that I feel toward repeat offenders, that family members and friends must feel when their loved ones revert back to the old ways of drugs and crime. And then your article showed that, at least in Anderson's case, there is hope—a bright side. "And every Sunday his mother's face glowed as he walked through the church door" (quoted from your article). I could just see the face of this woman as she saw her son— see the happiness, the hope, the love. And I thought of all the mothers who never experience this—rather they are taken to the morgue to see their son who has been murdered or killed as a result of his lifestyle.

Needless to say, there was a hush over the entire courtroom. I know there were tears in several eyes, including the two court clerks. I told Anderson he should be thankful that he had people who cared enough for him to stick by him, that many of those in the courtroom that day probably did not have anyone who cared what happened to them. I dismissed the violation of probation. And because of just a few such success stories, I shall continue to encourage and *order* probationers to get their high school diplomas, get jobs, go to rehabilitation, go to anger management seminars, or whatever else I feel would help them. It takes a little more time to be concerned, but I do want to be more than just a robot who hands out sentences.

Judge Pugh was right. I do have a caring family. My father and cousins knew to call on God in their time of need because of their mothers, who called His name feverishly when they were raising their sons. But they didn't stop there. They prayed even after they were gone. Fred's mother and grandmother also never stopped praying.

The last time I saw Anderson we talked about Harold, and he said something that stuck with me: "We all got him high."

That's true. Little did he and my other cousins know when they laughed and watched Harold get high years ago that they were sending him on a path of destruction. But we both agreed it wasn't too late to alter the course. Harold is still alive, and one thing is definite: It's better to pull him up as many times as necessary, than to have to lower him once six feet.

10

THE GREAT HUSH

The friendship that can cease
has never been real.
—SAINT JEROME

One day in the spring of 1991, Alex was in town visiting from his home in Knoxville, Tennessee. Oftentimes, when he'd be troubled or just needed to get away, he would come back to his native home and visit New Hope Church. It was a place to unload the stress and burdens of the week and allow the minister's sermon to serve as fuel to get through the next five days. Sometimes Fred would sing for Alex. His favorite song was "Hold to God's Unchanging Hand."

Alex was in town this time to continue interviewing his old buddy for a story about his life. He had always thought Fred was a fascinating man, and he felt the world would be inspired by his trials and triumphs. In order to get started on the book, he needed to gather some more information. But in the midst of the interviewing, the two got off on the strange subject of burial plots. He told Fred that when he passed, he wanted to be buried in the front yard of the Palmer House. He asked Fred to get the paperwork started, and he promised he would. At the time, Alex's request didn't seem too strange, because it was just general conversation. However, the next week, Fred did as he requested and started talking with state and museum officials.

The following month, Alex invited Fred and Ernestine to his home in Knoxville, just to get away and talk more about the book. While they were there, Ernestine mentioned that she would like to move, and she had looked at a few houses. She mentioned one in particular that she liked. Then out of the blue, Alex suggested that he buy the house for them. They both told him no, that was out of the question. But then they had forgotten about his character. He was a giving man, always looking to do something for others. For instance, when the filming of *Roots* started, Alex approached LeVar Burton, who played Kunta Kinte, and told him that the filming was an extraordinary time in his life and that his mother should be on hand to see it. When Burton told him he couldn't afford to send for his mother, Alex sent her a plane ticket.

Alex's generosity toward Fred was even stronger. Since they were boys, he had always seen Fred having to struggle. Now that they were older, and he was able to, Alex wanted to make sure Fred never had to struggle again. That's why Fred shouldn't have been surprised that on Alex's next visit to Henning he brought up the house issue again. Fred agreed that the house Ernestine liked— an old ten-room, Continental-style home—was beautiful. But when Alex again spoke of getting it, Fred refused. He had too much pride for that, even if Alex was like a brother to him. During his visit, Alex stopped by the museum to see Fred and talked with him about the house. Arthilia Sawyer, a worker at the museum and good friend to them both, overheard their conversation and pulled Fred to the side once Alex left the room.

"He really wants you to have that house, and he's not going to be satisfied until he gets it for you," she said. "So please say yes."

Fred thought some more and eventually came up with a compromise. After discussing it with Ernestine, Fred told Alex he would allow him to get the house, but he wanted to assume the payments at some point. Alex agreed, then said with a smile: "Well, I'm glad you did come around, because I've already gotten it."

When Fred and Ernestine moved into the house, people came from all over town to see it. Many couldn't understand such love between two people not of the same bloodline. But then, quite possibly, they didn't know the story that Fred once told Alex about the house, which probably fueled Alex's desire to buy it.

When Fred was a teenager, the house was owned by Jack Austin, the town boss and one of the men who would team up with Sam Thum to keep Fred from purchasing land from the railroad company. It was also the same house that a young Fred and young Ennis Reed were passing by one day when Mrs. Austin yelled out the door and asked them if they wanted to make a dime apiece. They both said yes. When they got up to the door, she told them to take off their shoes before they came in, then instructed them to move an old antique chest up a spiraling staircase to the second floor of the house. Needless to say, that chest was extremely heavy. But the two boys wanted the money. They moved the chest as instructed.

It's funny how life brings things back around, then adds a little twist. Not only did Fred go on to become the city's first black mayor, but he ended up living in the house of the town boss. Indeed, Alex was pleased with what he had done for his buddy. Unfortunately, he wouldn't be around long enough to see him enjoy it.

In February of 1992, Fred got a phone call informing him that Alex had suffered a massive heart attack and was dead. Like the call he'd gotten about the death of his son Henry, he just stood there in shock. It didn't really hit him that Alex was gone until he went to City Hall where a bunch of reporters and television crews were waiting to talk to him. When the first question about Alex's death was asked, Fred let go and cried uncontrollably. It hit him. His buddy was gone.

There were two memorial services, one in Memphis, Tennessee, and one in Henning, at New Hope. Fred hadn't planned to attend the one in Memphis, but the family—Alex's middle brother, George, and others—sent for Fred and Ernestine. Fred left word with some of the church members that when they saw the processional coming toward New Hope to start ringing the old town bell. When he and Alex were boys, the bell was rung when somebody died.

At the funeral in Memphis, Fred saw people from nearly every walk of life—African dignitaries, politicians, actors, and actresses. There was a spot in the program where he was asked to say something. He didn't know what to say, but then he heard George whisper, "Sing, Little Fred, sing." The only song he could think of was "Hold to God's Unchanging Hand." And he sang it as he never had before. The whole church was moved, to the point many stood up and sang along. When he finished, a white judge, Judge Willard Norvell, ran up to Fred and grabbed him in his arms. Crying, the judge said he'd never heard anything so moving.

After the service at New Hope, a flute player from Memphis who had studied African music led a processional from the church around the block to the Haley Museum where Alex had requested to be buried. Max Reynolds, a longtime white resident of Henning, saw the processional as it passed by. He said usually his dogs would bark and whine whenever the bell rang, but this time they didn't make a single sound. Oddly, he said, they stretched their little paws out and put their head down on top of them, almost as if paying respect. He said he couldn't even hear the birds chirping. And he was right. When the bell stopped ringing, there was a great hush, and all that could be heard was the flute player leading the way to the burial site of one of Africa's native sons—one of America's heroes.

While doing some research, I came across a book called *Black Light: The African American Hero.*

Created by director Bill Duke, with an introduction from actor Danny Glover, the photo-essay highlights a number of individuals who stand out in black history. Among them are Martin Luther King Jr., Langston Hughes, Malcolm X and his widow, Betty Shabazz, Maya Angelou, and, of course, Alex Haley. For a long time, such individuals seemed bigger than life, beyond my reach. They were people I saw on television, at the movies, in books. But being a journalist provided me an extension to actually contact them and to see that some are very personable. I remember talking to Betty Shabazz before her death and how kind she was during an interview about her late husband. Then there was the conversation with Danny Glover, who returned a phone call to my home after I left a message with his publicist. It was like talking to one of the fellows. He was very down to earth. But it was my correspondence with Maya Angelou that I remember the most.

I had started a magazine at college during my junior year, and I needed a judge for a poetry contest I was sponsoring. I always thought big. So I figured who better to judge than Maya Angelou. I got the address of the college where she taught and sent her a letter, not really expecting a prompt response. But within about a week, I received a letter back. She said she didn't have time to be a judge but wanted to contribute to the prize money. A check for $250 was enclosed. She also asked that I keep her informed regarding my life.

"I am convinced that you are going to do something marvelous," she wrote.

Not giving up on a judge, and still thinking big, I sent a letter to Nikki Giovanni. She wrote back and said she could judge the contest. I received the letters from these two great women back in the summer of 1990, and I still have them to this day. They are not only an inspiration, but a lesson that nothing's too big, and nothing or no one is out of reach.

However, when it comes to great individuals, it may not be necessary to go that far. They may be just a few miles away, around the corner, or right next door. In his introduction to *Black Light: The African American Hero,* Glover describes a hero as a person who transforms the hardship of his or her experience into a form of inspiration for others. In short, that person makes humanly possible what may seem impossible to some. One person that comes to mind is my cousin Vernice Armour, a twenty-nine-year-old combat helicopter pilot for the U.S. Marines. She flew numerous missions during Operation Iraqi Freedom in 2003, becoming the first black female fighter pilot for not only the Marines but the entire Department of Defense. Other heroes are our mothers, fathers, grandparents, teachers, everyday individuals. Irene Deaner, the grandmother of Harold's son, is one of them. She took on the responsibility of raising Devon and his seven other siblings after their mother, her daughter, an intravenous drug user, died at age twenty-nine. The children have four different fathers who don't provide much help. Irene gets some assistance, but most of the money to care for the children comes from her personal income, savings, and a few family members.

Then there are the men in my family, and those like them, who have overcome substance abuse. Using is easy. But it takes a real man to stop, fight through the urge, and never look back. Harold's father revived his old upholstery business and has a spot for his son when he gets out of prison. He hopes to one day give Harold the business. My cousin Anderson, who once pawned his sister's thirteen-thousand-dollar car for three rocks of cocaine, has a city job and is saving to buy a house. Another runs his own restaurant. And one cousin, who once showed me the holes in his arms from where he shot heroin, has a successful career in the military. Then there's my father, Lucas, after whom I'm proud to be named. He's retired from the school system after twenty-eight years of teaching, and he and my mother are living in a house built on land given to him by his father. The others have also found stability. They are all survivors, warriors.

This is just my family. But there are other success stories in families all over the world. Alex's book *Roots* portrayed the courage and strength of a family's survival despite slavery's horrific grip. The book inspired millions. There are stories today just as encouraging. That's why Alex wanted us to talk to elders like Fred Montgomery and Daddy Roy, storytellers in their own right who weathered the turbulent times of yesterday to provide a clearer and better today.

They are the iridescent magic of black light that shines in the dark, illuminating the way. They are heroes.

11

LIFE NOW

A lot has happened since Alex's death. If he were still alive, he would no doubt be moved by the accomplishment of his buddy, who at the age of eighty-four stepped down as mayor in June 2001 after serving twelve years. Fred's accomplishments during that time were numerous. Most notable was his effort in helping to unite Henning, which had kept schools segregated until the early 1970s. He also was instrumental in bringing a new factory to town, and he had new apartments built for low-income and elderly residents.

Several years back this town of Henning held a special program honoring Fred Montgomery for his many years of political and community service. Knowing Alex, he would have attended the program. A proclamation from the state legislature was read in his honor, and a number of people spoke about the impact he made on their lives. Some of the stories were humorous:

> Whenever he could, Fred tried to mentor the young black boys in the community. One of his biggest benefits was giving them part-time jobs in his plumbing business and teaching them a skill. On one occasion, he asked Robert, a boy who was working with him, to pass him a pipe. But Robert was slow to respond.
>
> "Did you hear me, boy? I said pass me that pipe," Fred ordered.
>
> When Robert failed to respond a second time, Fred told him he was going to fire him if he didn't do what he said. By this time, a girl had passed by, and Robert finally handed Fred the pipe.
>
> "I'm sorry, Mr. Fred," Robert said. "But you see, I split my breeches not too long ago while working. And that girl who just passed by, that was my girlfriend, and

if I had gotten the pipe for you right then, she would have seen my behind."

Chuckling to himself, Fred forgave the poor boy.

During the program others noted Fred's passion for the well-being of others, like the time he took two elderly brothers into his home. Both of the men were in their seventies and had become senile. One was going blind, and the other was just about deaf. The relative they lived with, who was taking care of them, had died, leaving them homeless. The men had grown up with Fred, and he couldn't rest until he knew they were in good hands. When he couldn't find anyone to care for them, he and Ernestine took them into their home and cared for them until the men died.

Then there was that January during his first year as mayor when a gas-line leak caused most of the town's residents to lose their heat. After the problem was fixed, Fred took it upon himself to visit the town's elderly and make sure the pilot light flame on their heaters was lit. When he entered the homes most of the residents were wrapped from head to toe in quilts and blankets yet were still trembling from the extreme cold. After restoring their heat, many of them cried and hugged Fred in relief. As he was leaving the home of one white woman, she walked him to the door and with tears in her eyes, asked him what was the charge. Fred looked at her smile, and the tears running down her reddening cheeks, now starting to get warm from the heat, and replied: "There's no charge. I'm getting my pay right now."

The stories of his love are many.

As Fred looked out across the audience of black and white faces that evening, he thought about the time those white boys rode their ponies through his friends' marble game, and he got so mad that he threw a rock and hit one of them in the back of the head. Whoever would have thought that the grandchildren of those boys, the grandchildren of residents who once called him "nigger," would grow up and address him as Mayor Montgomery. Fred believes God vindicates for us; all we have to do "is give our problems to Him." Now, much older and wiser, Fred gives his rocks to God.

"If we could wait a few seconds, instead of saying or doing something harsh to someone, then we'd probably be able to pass off whatever happened and move on," he says. "God wants us to be as patient with each other as He is with us."

As Fred's eyes continued to skim the audience that night, he was slightly disappointed by one face he didn't see—that of Rev. George Hart. He had telephoned and said he couldn't make it, but he promised to be there in spirit. However, Fred would have liked to see him one more time. He had run into Reverend Hart about a year before he stepped down as mayor.

He was paying a bill at the dentist's office when a bearded white man approached him and asked if he recognized him. The man looked familiar, but Fred wasn't sure. The man then said, "I was the one who pulled you out of the river, nearly thirty years ago." Fred moved a few steps closer, and sure enough, it was him. He didn't know who he was because of the hair on his face, and the added weight. They both embraced, and burst into tears. People in the waiting room who didn't even know what was going on became emotional just watching them. He told Fred he was in town seeing a friend and decided to visit the dentist for a quick checkup. Fred invited him to the house to see Ernestine. But before leaving the office, they both came to an eerie realization after glancing at the calendar on the receptionist's desk: Their reunion was the same day as the boating accident, the day he saved Fred's life.

While riding home from the ceremony honoring him, Fred passed the railroad tracks where he attempted to take his life. He thought once again about Reverend Hart; how he and his son had pulled him from the river, and how the pain of losing another son was so great that he wanted a train to end it all. Then he looked into Ernestine's beautiful eyes, at his son who was driving the car, and the white people waving as he passed by. And he thought: *God, how merciful you are. Thank you for sparing me.*

With tears in his eyes, he remembered when he was

little, and what his grandmother Callie told him one day while they were fishing. "There's going to be a better day."

She was right, Fred thought. And it felt good to be alive.

Since stepping down as mayor, Fred continues to be the curator and main tour guide at the Alex Haley Museum, sharing his stories like a faithful servant guided by a quiet voice from on high. The people come from everywhere, some by the busload. Children who don't like school or aren't making the grade are motivated to do better when they hear his childhood experiences. Countless adults are inspired by his triumph over adversity and often make return visits with others. He's constantly receiving letters from people who have visited the museum or read about him. One woman from Bristol, Virginia, saw a story about him that I had done for the AP in her local newspaper and wrote: "I'm sixty and have been in my small town since I was four. When I was in school I couldn't understand why all of us, white and black, couldn't eat, drink, and go to school together. This wasn't right. But through God's grace, hopefully we'll continue to improve. By the way, I'm white, but what difference does it make? God made us *all*."

I'm among those repeat visitors. Every time I visit home, I make time to see my old friend, still following and absorbing his wisdom at thirty-three. Sometimes I stay overnight with him and Ernestine.

"Only two writers have slept in that bed you're in,

and that's you and Alex," Fred said one night when I visited. "He stayed in this guest bedroom every time he came to see me. He was welcome, and so are you."

Each time I leave Fred, I can't help but think back to that first time he took me on a tour of the museum and I sat and talked with him afterward. I couldn't wait to tell others about him—his miraculous existence, his undying love and faith. I'm reminded of the story Holocaust survivor Corrie ten Boom had to tell.

During World War II, Corrie and her family risked their lives to help Jews escape from the Nazis by hiding them in their home. But the Nazi police eventually raided the home, and Corrie and her family were arrested and sent to different concentration camps, with Corrie and her sister, Betsie, going to Ravensbruck, one of the worst. But their spirits didn't succumb to the horrible conditions surrounding them. They read passages from a little Bible they had managed to smuggle into their barrack-room, lifting the spirits and increasing the faith of many other prisoners. Betsie died at the camp. But Corrie was released not long after. She later learned that her release had been a mistake. About a week after she was let go, all the women her age in the camp were killed. Corrie realized God had kept her alive for a reason. Before her death at age ninety-one, she began a worldwide ministry to more than sixty countries, telling everyone who would listen about what she and Betsie learned in Ravensbruck: "There is no pit so deep that God's love is not deeper still."

Fred was once in that pit, but God pulled him out. He will do the same for all of us, if we just have faith. That's what I tell people when I talk about Fred Montgomery, and what God has done for him.

✳   ✳   ✳

I truly believe that it was my faith, and a new, forgiving mind-set concerning white people that helped me through one of the more trying times in my life.

On Friday night, February 1, 2002, I was traveling down one of the streets leading out of the predominantly white suburb where I worked, when a police car put on its flashing lights and got in behind me. The speed limit was 40. My speedometer showed I was doing about 35 mph. What was the problem? I pulled over and the cop approached my window. He was a white man who appeared to be in his early to mid-forties. He said he'd pulled me over because my left taillight was out, and he just wanted to warn me. However, he proceeded to check my license. He seemed to be taking a long time, and I started to get a little nervous. When he returned, he asked me to get out and face the vehicle. It was then that he put my hands behind my back and started putting handcuffs on me. He said when he checked my license a green capias (arrest warrant) appeared, meaning an order had been issued for my arrest. When I asked what for, he said he didn't know, and that I'd have to find out once I got downtown. However, he seemed a bit puzzled that such an order had been issued even though I had a valid driver's license. I couldn't believe it was happening. I'd seen people handcuffed and pushed headfirst into police cars on television, but I never thought it would happen to me. What would be in store for me when I got downtown? What would people say once they found out I'd been arrested? But then I took a deep breath, exhaled slowly, and said to myself: "Everything is going to be all right. God will see to it."

When I got to the precinct, I discovered the green capias had been issued because I failed to appear in court. Then I remembered. Several months earlier, my license had been suspended because of several unpaid speeding tickets. I paid the tickets and got a new license, but I failed to appear before the judge to show proof of the new license, which prompted the green capias and my arrest. That was my fault. The penalty—two days in jail without bond.

I was placed in a holding cell that reeked of urine with about ten other guys, mostly black and Hispanic except for one white. The cell was only about ten feet by twelve feet, which meant there was little room to be comfortable. The toilet looked as though it hadn't been cleaned in weeks, if ever. I sat there for about three hours before my name was called, and I was moved to another, less-crowded, cell. The only other person in there with me was a short, dumpy, unshaven white man by the name of John Tango. It was his second time in. He, too, had missed a court date.

John said he had just gotten a job as a construction foreman and was afraid his arrest may have jeopardized his position. I hadn't given it a lot of thought, but my job might also be in jeopardy. My bosses had always been pretty down to earth and understanding. But two days in jail?

When I told John it was my first time in, he gave me some advice: "Mind your own business, and you'll be okay."

Of course, it wasn't anything I didn't know, but I appreciated him telling me anyway.

After waiting there several more hours, we were given the continental breakfast—bologna, light bread, cold grits, and warm juice. By this time I was starving, so I ate it—all of it. I was moved around about two more times before a nurse drew my blood, and I was taken to a larger area with steel benches in the center and cells lining the walls. Most of the cells were already occupied, so the new guys were given floor mats and placed wherever there was room. My cell contained two white men. One claimed to be Willie Nelson's cousin, and the other, who went by Bob, was a recovering alcoholic who was waiting to go before a judge for allegedly abusing his wife. Cousin Willie, a skinny, bearded dude who coughed profusely, was a cocaine addict. He said he'd been a big-time country singer in Nashville at one time and had made a lot of money. But he lost all of it because of his addiction, and now he lived on the streets. A lot of the inmates were homeless and saw jail as a refuge, like the Salvation Army. After all, they were fed three times a day and had a place to sleep out of the elements. I relaxed as best I could on the floor mat, my feet at the base of another grimy toilet, and my head near the cell's door. Cousin Willie and Bob slept in bunk beds.

Ironically, two men from the race I once hated were now my roommates.

Around six in the morning, I officially became an inmate of the Davidson County Jail. I was taken to the second floor where I signed a few forms, removed my clothes, showered, and then put on a bright orange jumpsuit with orange slip-on shoes trimmed in white. I was given what looked like a rectangular-shaped crate that contained some basic necessities—soap, tooth-brush, toilet paper, underwear, T-shirts, blanket—and moved to a gymnasium in the building with about thirty other inmates. There, each of us was given a plastic cot that resembled a small boat and a floor mat to go inside. The temperature outside was probably about forty-five degrees, and it had to be about forty in that gym. We complained, especially after two inmates had seizures as a result of the cold. But the security officer just said there was something wrong with the heating system, and that we'd have to make do. We were given extra wool blankets, which felt like sleeping under a large S.O.S pad. Nevertheless, I made do. That gym was going to be home until Monday morning.

Doing nothing was probably the toughest for me. Even though I had only two days, it seemed like for ever. I couldn't fathom staying months, or years, but brothers right there with me and elsewhere were doing it. I thought about my cousin Harold. In a weird sort of way, I kind of admired him. He would tell me in his letters that part of surviving behind bars was being mentally tough. I now understand. To help pass the time, I talked with some of the brothers. They reminded me of some of the guys from my old stomping ground, brothers who had the potential to make it out of the hood but somewhere life threw them a curveball.

One guy, who was in on a drug charge, as many were, managed to fix a malfunctioning phone in the gym by meticulously connecting certain wires, allowing inmates to call out. This guy could have been an electrical engineer. Then there was the brother who talked about past presidents and how they compared to the current one. He talked confidently about their administrations, as if he were getting the information directly from a book. He could have been a politician, or a history professor, but instead he ended up a convicted felon serving time for burglary. It reminded me of Sammy the Pimp and West Indian Archie in Alex Haley's *The Autobiography of Malcolm X*. Sammy was organized, and could have easily been some type of businessman outside the pimp game and peddling reefer. West Indian Archie, on the other hand, ran numbers and would have made a good accountant. But somewhere in their lives they got caught up in their environment, and with no strong influence to lead them to do what was right, resorted to lives of crime to survive. The brothers I saw were no different.

On Monday, the security officer walked into the gym around 10:00 a.m. and called my name. As I gathered my blankets to turn them in, John asked if I would contact his brother for him. John suffered from high blood pressure and had to be rushed to the hospital the day before for stabilization. He was having trouble contacting his lawyer and wanted his brother to try. I told him I would help him, and we shook hands. During our conversations, I had told John my profession, so as I was leaving he quipped: "I'm sure you'll write about this someday."

I smiled.

When I got home, I contacted my editor. Jacques, a good friend who retrieved my car to prevent it from being towed after the arrest, had called the bureau early Saturday and told them what happened. But I wanted to provide the details. To my relief, my editor understood and was sympathetic. I then made the call

John requested. His brother was glad to know he was all right, and said he would contact John's lawyer. It felt good to help him.

A few months later, I told my experience to a black policeman who'd become a good friend of mine, and I also talked to a supervisor in the Davidson County Criminal Court Clerk's office. Both agreed that because I had a valid driver's license when I was pulled over by the officer, I shouldn't have been arrested, even though I didn't show up in court. They said I had a possible case, and they wouldn't blame me if I contacted a lawyer. But I didn't think any vindication was necessary, because I believe God allowed the incident to happen for a reason, to open my eyes even more.

After seeing those men in jail, and pondering how different their lives could have been with more positive intervention during childhood, I was motivated to work at a group home for troubled teens called Youth Emergency Services of Middle Tennessee. By sharing some of my experiences, and telling them about the men in my family who overcame adversity, I hoped to provide them with the fortitude to stay on the straight and narrow path. But I also wanted them to realize the consequences of straying. I orchestrated a trip to the Riverbend Maximum

Security Institution in Nashville, home to some of the most ruthless criminals. While there, the boys from the group home heard from a robust inmate named Ben who was serving a life sentence for murder.

"It's not the big things that I miss, but the little things," Ben said. "What I wouldn't give to sleep in my own bed, to push a shopping cart in a grocery store and pick out the food I want. But I lost my freedom. I'm told not only what to eat, but when to go to sleep, and when to get up. Straighten up, boys. You don't want to come in here."

What Ben said that day didn't just rattle the youth with me. I, too, was touched by the reality of his words. A lot of times we take our freedom for granted. But as I walked out the prison gates, passing the razor-wire fence towering on either side of me, I realized Ben and many others wouldn't see freedom for years, if ever. Once outside the prison, I thought about the day I was released from the Davidson County Jail, and how comfortable it felt to sleep in my own bed again and eat food I wanted. But more important, I was thankful to God for His mercy, for sparing me. Because that first weekend in February of 2002, I saw what might have happened if I had smoked with my cousins years ago. I saw robbers and addicts. I saw me.

12

THE GOOD

Find the good and praise it.
—ALEX HALEY

Years have passed since I first met Fred Montgomery, but I must admit I'm still mystified when I think about how our paths crossed and I came to write about his life. Was it fate? Were some of the things that happened in my life leading to our meeting? I dodged a life of substance abuse and crime. I wanted to be a pilot, but I ended up a writer. My grandmother would always say, "God is going to use you for something." Then there was Maya Angelou, who believed I'd "do something marvelous." Well, I don't know about all that, but I do know I'm a better person because of Fred. His life gave me a credible blueprint on how to deal with life's problems and even grow stronger from them. As I listened to his words of wisdom, I noticed there were some things I'd heard before, but forgotten for whatever reason. However, if we're fortunate, God will send someone our way to remind us of how He wants us to live. In many cases, that person is wiser and much older, like our elders; someone who's been refined by life's trials and tribulations, instead of tarnished by them. Throughout all Fred's struggles and tragedies, he managed to find love and courage, forgiveness, and faithfulness. But most of all, he firmly embraced the latter—like a modern-day Job.

I remember his telling me that when he was in his fifties a doctor discovered blood in his urine. But Fred didn't become flustered. Instead, he got down on his knees and asked God to "fix whatever is wrong." After he got up, he had a strange urge to go into the kitchen and drink two glasses of water. When he went to the bathroom the next morning, there was no trace of blood. His doctor also couldn't find any. The more Fred told me about such experiences and other adversity he'd overcome, the more I understood why Alex Haley wanted to write a book about him. Alex would often say, "Find the good and praise it." He definitely found the good in Fred. But I saw an even deeper meaning to Alex's statement when I came across

Galatians 5:22–24 in the King James Version of the Bible: "But the fruit of the Spirit is love, joy, peace, longsuffering, gentleness, goodness, faith, meekness, temperance: against such there is no law."

In searching for the good, we are actually seeking the fruits of the Spirit, a relationship with God—a friendship. This is the spiritual bond Fred, my father, his father, and the other men in my family had that allowed them to know who to call on in their time of need, when no one else seemed to be of help. I now have that relationship. However, like most men, I used to be stubborn. I became distracted during college and prayed less and less. It was hard for me to kneel and talk to someone I couldn't see. But now, thanks to Fred and the miracles he shared with me, I have a strong faith. I pray and read my Bible. Things have happened in my life—positive things. I no longer feel hatred or boil over with anger. I'm more compassionate. But most of all, I'm forgiving. The bitterness I once harbored over my father's broken promises, and the time we didn't spend together because of his alcoholism, has been replaced with the joy of having him in my life clean and sober. We now spend more time together. I even convinced him to do something I thought he'd never do with me. My father very rarely went to the movies. Whenever he'd come to visit, and I'd offer to treat him to the latest feature, he would turn me down.

But during a visit home on January 25, 2003, I asked my father to join me, my mother, and my two sisters in seeing the *Antwone Fisher* story. He said no at first. But when we were close to leaving, I went to his bedroom, and there he sat in his coat and hat. When I asked where he was going, he replied: "With you."

That was the first movie my father, sixty-eight, had gone out to see in nearly thirty years. And he enjoyed it. We all did, as a family.

Now that my father's fully back in my life, I don't hesitate to say "I love you" and tell him how much I appreciate him, because I realize how fortunate I am. Many young men are fatherless. I also have a better sense of who I am, a completeness that encompasses confidence and responsibility. Who knows? I may finally be ready for that special person.

At the time this book was completed, Fred and Ernestine had been married sixty-seven years. My father's mother and father were married sixty-three years before my grandfather's death. Fred told me prayer and communication were the key to their relationship's longevity. My grandfather had told me the same. I watched one day as Fred and Ernestine interacted with each other. They laughed and talked, enjoying the simplicity of each other's presence. Later that evening, Fred told me that another part of his marital success was "seeing the inner beauty."

"Ernestine and I are old and wrinkled. I mean look at her over there; she can hardly get out of that chair," he said with a slight chuckle. "But when I look at her, she's as beautiful as when we first met. You know why? I'm looking on the inside."

That's what I didn't do with the woman to whom I was once engaged. I was engrossed in her attractiveness. But if I had taken time to look beyond that, I would have seen our incompatibility and saved us both heartache. I talked with several young men who had similar experiences. They all said that once they let go of their egos, humbled themselves, and began to pray for direction, they were able to find their mate for life. And if infidelity should rear its ugly head, they knew to whom to turn to help them squash it. The mate God chooses will play a role in your spiritual well-being. A person not of the same yoke who is argumentative and causes constant tension might drive one to sin. Fred shared with me 2 Corinthians 6:14: "Do not be yoked together with unbelievers. For what do righteousness and wickedness have in common? Or what fellowship can light have with darkness?" (NIV).

Even more, if I'm blessed to have a son, and he should ask me one day what type of woman to marry, I want to be able to say without hesitation: "Someone like your mother."

Indeed, I'm wiser now when it comes to finding that significant other. But because of the increasingly violent world in which we live, I found myself going back and forth on the issue of marriage and having children. At one point, I decided I didn't want to be a father. There were several factors that caused me to feel that way. But then Fred helped me see the good. Several things helped to change my mind. One was the death of seven-year-old Jake Joyner, a little boy who was getting his hair cut in my cousin's barbershop when he was fatally shot during a botched robbery. Shortly after that, it was the Oklahoma City bombing, in which many innocent children lost their lives. Then came the terrorist attacks on September 11, 2001, which killed hundreds and left just as many little boys and girls without a mother or father to tuck them in at night. In an e-mail to all Associated Press employees concerning 9/11, company president Lou Boccardi wrote: "These are difficult and dangerous days." But as I had done so many times before, I went to Fred like a child seeking consolation from an older loved one, and his wisdom once again comforted me. He reminded me of the Middle Passage, and how one out of every four slaves on the ships died. He said they also risked death almost every day on plantations in the new land. But many remained prayerful and hopeful. Even though life was threatened, those faithful didn't stop having babies. They just put their trust in God and gave their children as much love as possible until death, whenever that might be.

We live in an unfair world, but just because life is taken away doesn't mean we should stop giving it. Sadly, there will probably be more terrorist attacks and wars, as well as kidnappings, murders, and other terrible acts in our very communities. Those who do evil want to disrupt our lives. However, their attempts are foiled when we pick ourselves up and move on. God has reasons for doing everything, reasons our finite minds don't understand. For instance, why would He let hundreds die in the terrorist attacks, yet spare the lives of nine miners in Somerset County, Pennsylvania, who were trapped at least 250 feet underground for more than three days? There's no sure answer, but there was one definite outcome. The attacks united America and caused those who didn't believe in God or had lost faith to flock to their nearest churches to seek His mercy and salvation. Hundreds lost their lives, but millions were saved. A Michigan man probably said it best in the aftermath: "Although some lives are taken, and some are rescued, the Lord's in control of all things for good."

This goodness was made plain to me while watching one of the events held around the nation to commemorate the first-year anniversary of the attacks. I saw Americans' indisputable commonality. At Ground Zero in New York City, the place where the World Trade Center once stood and where the most people died, families and friends—blacks, whites, Hispanics, Asians, and other races—gathered to remember those they lost. There was no hatred, no racism, just tears of sorrow all flowing into a melting pot of grief. Like the ocean that's the same color as far as the eye can see, those people were also the same—under the skin.

✳ ✳ ✳

Fred's stories about his hatred toward white people and the events that took place to change the way he felt were medicine for my soul. I thought long and hard about his realization that not all whites hated, and many were also capable of loving and caring. Additionally, those who may have had hatred in their hearts could change. For instance, Fred later learned that it was Sam Thum who recommended him to the Pipkin family as a worker in their store.

"Fred is good help, and honest," Thum told the family.

After learning what Thum had said, Fred thought about that time he helped him change the disc on the plow. And it became even more apparent to him that no matter how mean or ornery a person might be, God has planted a seed of good in each of us. But in order to make it grow we must water it with His love, thus changing our hearts. Fred shared the story of one white man who allowed God to come into his life, inspiring him to write a song for the ages.

John Newton had lived a life at sea since age eleven. His mother prayed for him to be a minister, teaching him the scriptures at an early age. But Newton desired to be a sailor, like his father. And he became one of the most ruthless. Slave-trading was his specialty.

On one particular voyage, Newton's ship got caught in a fierce storm. It ripped the vessel's canvas sails and splintered the wood on one side of the ship. It seemed doomed. Fearing for his life and the lives of his crew, Newton remembered his mother's prayers and the scriptures she taught him. In a cry of desperation, he yelled, "Lord, have mercy upon us." God spared Newton's life that day. Humbled by the experience, he reflected on God's mercy, and wrote: "Thro' many dangers, toils and snares, I have already come; 'tis grace has bro't me safe thus far, and grace will lead me home."

These words became part of the beloved song Newton would later pen—"Amazing Grace."

After his deliverance, Newton eventually got out of the slave trade and fulfilled his mother's wish. He became a minister and preached heavily against slavery. As a matter of fact, his thoughts were very influential in securing British abolition of the abhorrent practice.

Up until his death at the age of eighty-two, Newton never ceased to be amazed by the transforming power of God's grace. He told his friends before he died: "My memory is nearly gone, but I remember two things: that I am a great sinner, and that Christ is a great Savior."

In dealing with white people, I had let my sinful nature get the best of me. Fred's peaceful reasoning made me look in the mirror and accept what I had been doing. In a sense, I was no better than racist white people who feel most blacks are lazy and always looking for a hand up. I perpetuated the same stereotypical ideology by lumping them all under the category of "haters." But Fred changed that. I began to look for the good stories about white people, such as the one concerning Maryland linebacker Randy Earle, who was born a crack baby. The family of one of his white teammates and other residents in Farmingdale,

New York, helped raise him after his mother and father—both intravenous drug users—died of AIDS, which also claimed the lives of his little brother and sister. I also reflected on those white people who had assisted or influenced me in some way over the course of my life, like Carlie Ann Davis, my fifth-grade teacher who encouraged me to read and to realize I had the ability to become whatever or go wherever those books described.

There were others in high school and college, like my feature-writing instructor, Dr. Glenn Himebaugh. He helped hone my writing skills even more, which allowed me to get several internships and eventually gain the attention of Kent Flanagan, The Associated Press chief of bureau in Nashville who hired me right out of college. I didn't have a lot of experience, but he saw something in me and gave me a chance. There was Joe Edwards, whose consideration was key to my even meeting Fred. And then there was the caring letter from Judge Pugh concerning my cousin Anderson. If my initial feelings about white people hadn't been so saturated with hatred, I probably would have taken to heart one of the most profound statements ever made to me by a white person.

An AP photographer and I had gone to Carthage, Tennessee, the home of former vice president, Al Gore. It was 1992 and Bill Clinton, who had won the Democratic nomination, selected Gore to be his running mate. My assignment was to get reaction from the townsfolk. One of the people I talked to was Gore's second grade teacher, Eleanor Smotherman. She was close to ninety, and I was amazed at her sharpness. She was also very kind and peaceful. After the interview, I realized there was something I needed to clarify, so I called her back about an hour later. When she answered I told her my name and then said jokingly, in case she'd forgotten, that "I was the dark-skinned one." The photographer, Mark, was white. Her response was unexpected: "Young man, it doesn't matter what color you are, it's what you have upstairs." I didn't really expect her to say anything, let alone that. I had already judged her. Because of her age and the fact that she lived in a rural town, I assumed she was among those old white women who refused to divorce segregation and remained married to Jim Crow. But Ms. Smotherman, now deceased, was different, open-minded.

When I reflect, I realize all these white people

were placed in my life for a reason, and I remember the lesson Fred said he learned after the white minister and his son pulled him from the freezing river.

"Whoever God chooses to send his blessing by, receive it regardless of what color the messenger is, and be thankful for it."

But I also learned another lesson—the age of the messenger doesn't matter either. On one of my visits to the Alex Haley Museum, I brought a special person with me for Fred to inspire. That person would also play a part in my getting rid of years of guilt.

I was touched by Fred's desire to help others, in particular the two elderly men he took into his home and cared for until they died. I felt it was time for me to reach out, so I got in contact with Harold's son, Devon. Harold had started calling me at least once a month from prison, and he told me Devon was a sharp young man. But I didn't realize just how together he was until I talked with him. And when I saw him, his resemblance to his father was striking—the eyes, the nose, the way he walked. Despite having to help his grandmother take care of his now seven other younger siblings, the seventeen-year-old had made the honor roll several times, was a leader in his ROTC class, and found time to write poetry. When he told me that, I thought he might get some ideas from Fred's stories. But even more, as a young man I believed this wise old man was just somebody he should know.

When we got to the museum, Fred took him on a tour. Watching Devon hang on Fred's every word and seeing his eyes widen as he looked around the museum made me think about the images that had stayed with me—the picture of the griot and the boy standing behind him, cast members like James Earl Jones, Binter Kinte's piercing eyes, Alex Haley looking out over the ocean from a dock in Annapolis, Maryland. At the end of the tour, Devon walked up to me and said, "Thank you," a big smile on his face. He said Fred had inspired him, and that he now had a lot to write about. His enlightenment was evident in the words of a poem he wrote:

Who am I? That's the question I would ask when I looked in the mirror. Some days he looked as though his world was falling apart. . . . Then he remembered the words of an old wise man. . . . Ancestors determined to push forward, to become doctors, lawyers, teachers, writers, mayors. Now I know the person in the mirror. He's been inside all along, a fighter. He's a reflection of those who paved the way before him. Because of them, I am.

I beamed at his newfound enthusiasm. His words, and the expression on his face, let me know he was going to be all right. Suddenly, my years of guilt seemed to disappear. I was making up for the time I sat and did nothing while his father got high. But this time there was no cloud of smoke, and I could clearly see Devon heading in the right direction. I would be there to make sure he stayed the course. I was doing something—something good.

That evening, I left Fred and Devon alone and walked around to the front of the museum where Alex is buried. On his headstone is a list of his published and unpublished works. At the bottom is Fred Montgomery. I thought about those interviews Alex had with his old buddy, and his strong desire to tell the world about Fred's life, his faith, his love. Now, years later, his story is being told.

As I stood there over the grave of the great storyteller, a feeling of gratefulness, of completeness, consumed me. And at that moment, I envisioned myself walking down that dock, tapping Alex on the shoulder and saying:

"Here it is. You don't have to look any further. This is the book about your boyhood friend, the one who touched your life and has touched mine. Now, through this book, his life will enrich the lives of many."

I found him. The griot of Henning.

Appendix

"Crack in the Family"
(Essence, August 1992)

I knew my cousin Anderson pretty well when I was growing up. Because I have no brothers, he was like my big brother, and I always wanted to do everything he did and go everywhere he went.

I would watch him and his friends when they got together. They would sit around, shoot the breeze, smoke some marijuana. To me, it seemed harmless. But I never tried it, nor would my cousin let me.

I always asked him why he smoked it. He would simply say that it made him feel good, and then, ironically, he would threaten me: "If I ever catch you smoking marijuana, I'll kill you." Then he would take another long drag of a marijuana cigarette. Later the marijuana gave way to crack cocaine.

Anderson chose drugs as a momentary escape from the ghetto. He saw young men dying from cold-blooded shootings, overdoses and fights in the streets. I saw young men going to college and aspiring to become doctors and lawyers.

I felt like an Army dropout telling a Vietnam hero he didn't win the war. After all, what could I say? My cousin was fighting a war I knew nothing about, and he was losing.

At one point, Anderson actually enlisted in the Army for four years, and his life took a brief change for the better. I rejoiced. His return home was even more glorious. He looked like a new man when he arrived at the airport. His sister and I were elated.

Everything was fantastic for about a year. Then the entire environmental picture was redrawn—hanging out on the corner with old buddies, smoking marijuana, drinking liquor. But marijuana was not enough. Anderson had to find what all his friends were talking about. He had to find that "white girl"—cocaine.

When he found her, the symptoms came one after the other, as if he were suffering from some consuming disease. Anderson started by using half of his paycheck to buy rocks (crack, a solidified form of cocaine). Then he started spending his entire check. And when the money ran out, he pawned whatever he could get his hands on, even his mother's brass lamps.

I returned home from college to find a stranger.

Anderson wasn't the same person I had seen only a year before. He had lost weight, his color was darker, and he sounded insincere and hopeless. What could I say to him? He was 30 years old; I was a 19-year-old college student.

But my heart was filled with love, and my hand reached out, for this was the man I had adopted as my brother. I knew the old Anderson, and I wanted him back. I asked him to quit drugs. He promised he would.

Prayers and words of caution, however, mean nothing to a man consumed in his own smoke-filled world. Anderson was arrested, finally, for stealing.

But my family's love runs deep. Anderson was bailed out of jail and placed in a veterans' rehabilitation center. But although he spent several months in counseling, a week after his release he was back on the streets, doing the same old thing. This time his only brother reached out and took my cousin into his home, only to have his hand slapped. Anderson robbed him.

Yet his brother did not put him out. He stuck by him even more. He knew Anderson was knocking on death's door. Fortunately, a higher being opened another door first. Anderson's brother was able to persuade him to attend church.

At first it was only through his family's urging that Anderson went to church. But after a while he started going every Sunday without a word being said to him.

And every Sunday his mother's face glowed as he walked through the church door.

Now, thirty-four-year-old Anderson is celebrating more than a year of being drug-free and has a full-time job. He is attending church regularly, and he has assumed special roles in the church. In addition, he is actively playing a major role in helping others break their addiction to crack.

The last time I saw my cousin, I almost cried tears of joy. He was a fuller, livelier man, a man at whose courage I marveled. We talked for a long time. And before we finished he said to me, "If I ever see you using crack, I'll kill you."

I laughed, joyously.